# THE JOSIAH MACY, JR. FOUNDATION
## 1930-1955

*A Review of Activities*

NEW YORK
SIXTEEN WEST FORTY-SIXTH STREET
1955

KATE MACY LADD
From a portrait by Adele Herter

# OFFICERS AND STAFF

## 1955

WILLARD C. RAPPLEYE, M.D.
*President*

EDWIN S. S. SUNDERLAND
*Secretary*

CLARENCE G. MICHALIS
*Treasurer*

THE HANOVER BANK
*Assistant Treasurer*

FRANK FREMONT-SMITH, M.D.
*Medical Director and Executive Secretary*

DORA C. LISSEMORE
*Assistant for Grant-in-Aid Program*

RUTH ELIZABETH RUE
*Assistant for Conference Program*

o

# PAST DIRECTORS

| | |
|---|---|
| CHESTER H. ALDRICH* . . . . . . | 1930-1938 (Deceased, 1940) |
| WALTER C. ALVAREZ, M.D. . . . . | 1930-1932 |
| JOHN DEWEY, PH.D.* . . . . . . | 1930-1944 (Deceased, 1952) |
| FREDERIC J. FAULKS* . . . . . . | 1930-1933 (Deceased, 1933) |
| NELLIS B. FOSTER, M.D.* . . . . . | 1930-1933 (Deceased, 1933) |
| HAMILTON HADLEY* . . . . . . | 1930-1930 |
| LUDWIG KAST, M.D.* . . . . . . | 1930-1941 (Deceased, 1941) |
| JAMES F. MCKERNON, M.D.* . . . | 1930-1933 (Deceased, 1949) |
| J. NOEL MACY* . . . . . . . . | 1930-1931 |
| VALENTINE E. MACY, JR.* . . . . . | 1930-1931 |
| DAVE HENNEN MORRIS* . . . . . | 1930-1944 (Deceased, 1944) |
| STEWART PATON, M.D.* . . . . . | 1930-1938 (Deceased, 1942) |
| SAMUEL G. TREXLER, D.D.* . . . . | 1930-1949 (Deceased, 1949) |
| J. MACY WILLETS* . . . . . . . | 1930-1940 (Deceased, 1940) |
| ROBERT E. ALLEN . . . . . . . | 1931-1947 |
| DEAN SAGE . . . . . . . . . | 1932-1943 (Deceased, 1943) |
| PAUL H. SMART . . . . . . . . | 1933-1943 |
| WILLIAM W. HOPPIN . . . . . . | 1935-1940 (Deceased, 1948) |
| STANHOPE BAYNE-JONES, M.D. . . . | 1938-1941<br>1948-1954 |
| CHARLES SIDNEY BURWELL, M.D. . . | 1938-1942 |
| WILLIAM R. BIGGS . . . . . . . | 1941-1942 |

* Founder member.

ix

# PAST OFFICERS AND STAFF

*President*

LUDWIG KAST, M.D. . . . . . . . . . . . 1930-1941*

*Secretary*

J. NOEL MACY . . . . . . . . . . . 1930-1931

J. MACY WILLETS . . . . . . . . . . . 1931-1940*

*Treasurer*

VALENTINE E. MACY, JR. . . . . . . . . . 1930-1931

ROBERT E. ALLEN . . . . . . . . . . . 1931-1942

PAUL H. SMART . . . . . . . . . . . 1942-1943

*Executive Secretary*

COLONEL MARLBOROUGH CHURCHILL . . . . . 1930-1934*

*Assistant to the President and Executive Secretary*

HERBERT N. SHENTON, PH.D. . . . . . . . 1934-1936*

LAWRENCE K. FRANK . . . . . . . . . 1936-1938

*Executive Vice-President and Executive Secretary*

LAWRENCE K. FRANK . . . . . . . . . 1938-1941

*Director of the Medical Division*

WARD J. McNEAL, M.D. . . . . . . . . . 1931-1936

*Assistant for the Conference Program*

JANET FREED LYNCH . . . . . . . . . . 1948-1954

---

* Deceased.

# CONTENTS

# FOREWORD

THE FIRST of the Macy family to settle on the North American continent brought two British traditions that were to shape the careers of his male descendants: seafaring and public service. Thomas Macy and his wife, of Chilmark, Wiltshire, England, lived in Newbury, Massachusetts, from 1635 to 1639, and then moved to Salisbury, where Thomas served as town administrator for several terms. It must have been love of the sea and a venturesome spirit that led this first American Macy down the long Massachusetts coastline to join nine other colonists in the purchase of Nantucket Island  Here he continued to hold public office and established a family whose menfolk since then have distinguished themselves first in the coastal trade and the whaling industry, and later in commerce, finance, and philanthropy.

In the early years of the nineteenth century, when the family interests had expanded considerably, the young Josiah was making voyages to England and to the Mediterranean in his own ships carrying his own merchandise. The War of 1812 crippled American shipping for a time, but with the return of peace, transoceanic trade developed rapidly, as also did the Macy shipping and mercantile interests. In 1828, the firm of Josiah Macy and Son was established as a shipping and commission business in New York City. The first son in the enterprise was William Henry (four others joined later), whose son, Josiah, Jr., was born in 1838.

Josiah Macy and Sons entered the new and growing oil industry in the 1860's, acquiring an interest in the four-year-old Long Island Oil Company in 1867. The company's large refinery at Hunter's Point soon attracted the notice of John D. Rockefeller's lieutenants. In 1872, the Long Island Company

1

joined the Standard Oil group; thenceforward the Macy family fortunes were closely identified with that organization.

Josiah, Jr. entered the family business after his education at the Friends' School in New York and embarked upon a distinguished career as industrialist and banker. With business acumen he combined a sense of responsibility for the wise and public-spirited use of wealth. He gave wholeheartedly of his money and his services to hospitals and welfare organizations in the city, earning the gratitude and affection of a wide circle of his fellow citizens.

The youngest of the three children of Josiah Macy, Jr., and his wife, Caroline Louise Everit of Brooklyn, was Kate, who married Walter Graeme Ladd. Inheriting from both mother and father the Quaker traditions of simplicity, sincerity, and devotion to the service of mankind, the young woman early in her life took up the family's philanthropic habits. Though ill health curtailed her activities for many years, she contributed to hospitals, schools, settlements, and many institutions serving human needs.

Mrs. Ladd's experience with giving convinced her that organized philanthropy is more effective than scattered support of worthy causes. Her long illness turned her thoughts to the importance of good health and to the accomplishments and potentialities of medical research. Fortunately she became acquainted with Dr. Ludwig Kast, a Vienna-born physician with a background in practice and research. Dr. Kast's vision and wisdom gave clarity to her purpose. At her request, he made a critical survey of the status and trends of medical research and the most promising opportunities for assisting its progress.

With this survey as a basis, and with Dr. Kast's imaginative and sound thinking to guide her, Mrs. Ladd made her plans for a foundation to promote human welfare by means of assistance to scientific medicine and improved health care. She named the new foundation in memory of her father, and

2

endowed it with a liberal initial gift. With the wisdom of a true philanthropist, she outlined her wishes clearly in a letter of gift,* but gave her trustees enough freedom to enable them to adapt the Foundation's program to the changing needs of medicine and health. Broadly as she saw the whole subject of health, she understood that new knowledge constantly alters the direction of man's efforts to make his life more useful and satisfying. She wanted alert, informed persons, unfettered by instructions from out of the past, to make use of her gifts for the benefit of mankind.

While she lived, Mrs. Ladd followed the activities of the Foundation with unflagging interest. She generously added to her original gift, and left the Foundation a substantial amount at her death in 1945.

Dr. Kast logically became the Foundation's first President. Through the first eleven years of its existence he devoted his great resources of professional knowledge, his sound judgment, philosophic outlook, and understanding of organization procedure to the guidance of the enterprise. Through it, his ideals of service to medical science were translated into action.

In August, 1941, Dr. Kast died. Dr. Willard C. Rappleye, a member of the Board of Directors since 1933, succeeded to the presidency. His broad experience in medical education and administration, his understanding of the responsibilities and opportunities of the physician as a servant of mankind, his enthusiastic acceptance of Mrs. Ladd's views of the use to be made of her benefactions have insured continuance of the work so well begun by his predecessor.

CLARENCE G. MICHALIS
*Chairman of the Board of Directors*

---

* See pages 5, 6.

# AT THE QUARTER-CENTURY MARK

A survey of organized philanthropy made before the establishment of the Macy Foundation in April, 1930, revealed that in the field of medicine and public health far more aid was being given to biochemical and physiological research than to psychobiological and sociological, and that little effort was being made to synthesize old and new data derived from the highly specialized researches and new techniques. There was little systematic research into the interrelations between mind and body functions, and not much thought for the need to approach medical and health problems from the psychosocial point of view. An inviting prospect lay before a venturesome philanthropist: assistance to research in the basic medical sciences with extension into the study of psychosomatic and psychosocial problems.

Guided by the findings of the survey, Mrs. Walter Graeme Ladd made her plans for a new foundation. She wrote to the trustees who were to administer her gift: "It is my desire that the Foundation . . . should concentrate on a few problems rather than support many undertakings, and that it should primarily devote its interest to the fundamental aspects of health, of sickness, and of methods for the relief of suffering, in particular to such special problems in medical sciences, medical arts, and medical education as require for their solution studies and efforts in correlated fields as well. such as biology and the social sciences. To these ends the Foundation might give preference . . . to integrating functions in medical sciences and medical education for which there seems to be particular need in our age of specialization and technical complexities. Believing, as I do, that no sound structure of social or cultural welfare can be maintained without health, that

5

health is more than freedom from sickness, that it resides in the wholesome unity of mind and body, I hope that your undertaking may help to develop more and more in medicine, in its research, education, and ministry of healing, the spirit which sees the center of all its efforts in the patient as an individuality."

Instead of setting up new institutions or agencies, Mrs. Ladd preferred that the Foundation co-operate with appropriate existing agencies to support the development of integrating ideas and methods, "in seeking out promising new paths of approach to a better understanding and a wiser direction of human affairs concerned with social-minded health-care and education.

"Experience seems to show that in an enlightened democracy, private organized philanthropy serves the purposes of human welfare best, not by replacing functions which rightfully should be supported by our communities, but by investigating, testing, and demonstrating the value of newer organized ideas for sustained undertakings from which may gradually emerge social functions which in turn should be taken over and maintained by the public. I hope, therefore, that the Foundation will take more interest in the architecture of ideas than in the architecture of buildings and laboratories."*

So it came about that the Foundation entered upon its program at the beginning of the great depression and at a time when the nation's two hundred-odd foundations had turned to the relatively small grant in aid of a project and to fellowship programs in general preference to the large gift for endowment to university or research institution. The new group of trustees, with abundant opportunities to carry out Mrs. Ladd's wishes, found the grant-in-aid policy best suited to their task.

---

* For an account of the preliminary survey and definition of the Foundation's program, see: *Josiah Macy, Jr. Foundation, A Review by the President of Activities for the Six Years Ended December 31, 1936,* New York, 1937, 13-27.

6

In the twenty-five years of the Foundation's existence, its Directors have kept in mind Mrs. Ladd's dynamic concept of a foundation's role: full partnership, by support, encouragement, and suggestion, with the scholars who explore the outermost boundaries of knowledge.

Scientific research is supported in the United States by universities, the federal government, large and small privately endowed foundations, national organizations whose funds come in response to public appeals, and the great industries. A foundation of modest resources has ample opportunity to assist in areas not pre-empted by any of these organizations.

The United States government entered the field of medical and public health research in 1887, when the Public Health Service's Hygienic Laboratory was established. With the creation of the National Institute of Health in 1930, government participation in medical and health activities expanded rapidly; in 1935, the National Security Act more than doubled government expenditures for these purposes. At the beginning of the war of 1941-1945, the medical branches of the armed services and other government agencies, co-ordinated through the Committee on Medical Research of the Office of Research and Development, embarked upon a vast program of research upon problems important to national defense. Much of the program was conducted by means of grants-in-aid to universities and research institutions. In 1944, for example, the government spent ten million dollars on research in medicine. Contrary to expectation, the end of the war did not bring retrenchment, but rather a continuing rise in the sums devoted by government to scientific research. In 1952 the total had reached some seventy-three million dollars for medical research alone.* The 83rd Congress increased the 1954-55 appropriation for the seven National Institutes of Health of

---

* Ladimer, Irving, "Trends in Support and Expenditures for Medical Research, 1941-52," *Public Health Reports*, U. S. Department of Health, Education, and Welfare, 1954, *69*, 111-122.

the Public Health Service by more than ten million dollars above the President's request, to a total of $81,268,000.* The year before it had appropriated $71,218,000 — nearly five million dollars more than the amount requested.

Through private fund-raising organizations the citizens of the nation have given huge sums for research in the fields of cancer, heart diseases, infantile paralysis, multiple sclerosis, and others. Though much of the research supported by these foundations is of the target variety — projects aimed at finding the answers to specific problems in prevention and treatment of certain diseases — programs of basic research and of assistance to medical education have been initiated and carried through by them.

The endowed foundation, unlike government agencies and fund-raising foundations, is under no obligation to show immediate results. It is free to give assistance to basic research, to long-range programs which, though frequently revealing useful knowledge during their progress, may not reach their goals for many years. Often the original goal of an investigation becomes radically changed as new data, methods, and inspiration alter the scientist's view.

Also in the special province of the endowed foundation is sponsorship of research in previously unexplored areas and development of new instruments and techniques. The independent foundation can risk money on an untested concept that may open new windows on the scientific scene or may lead only to a blank wall. Such gambles have led to some of the greatest achievements of modern science.

Throughout the free world for centuries the university has been the sanctuary of scholarship and the natural habitat of basic research. It provides personnel, facilities, and stimulating environment for research. The partnership between university and foundation is truly mutual: the foundation furnishes

---

* The National Institutes of Health conduct and support research in cancer, mental health, heart diseases, dentistry, arthritis and metabolic diseases, microbiology, and neurological diseases.

8

material and moral support to the university investigator; the university and the investigator make it possible for the foundation to fulfill its mission. Recipient and grantor share responsibility and opportunity in equal measure. Awareness of this mutuality disposes of a sense of obligation on the part of the investigator and his institution toward the foundation and leads to genuine co-operation.

During its first quarter-century the Macy Foundation has fostered certain specific developments: first, the wider recognition of the psychosomatic approach in medicine; increase of research in problems of aging with the resulting change in public attitude toward the needs and rights of the older citizen; use of the technique of the small, multiprofessional conference as a means of communication among workers in the various branches of science; the application of mental health principles to problems of understanding among individuals and groups; research in and integration of approach to problems in medical and health-care administration. The Foundation's assistance has helped produce contributions to knowledge in such areas as diseases of the circulatory system (arteriosclerosis, heart disease, hypertension, shock); problems of nutrition (deficiency in vitamin A, the nature and role of the vitamin B complex, vitamin C, and biotin in nutrition); growth and development; personality development; endocrine physiology and pathology (adrenal cortex, anterior pituitary gland); physiology of bone. The breadth of scope of the earlier activities of the Foundation now affords ample opportunity to serve medical research through synthesis of information in widely divergent areas of knowledge.

The Macy Foundation has supported research and integration of research activities at the level of intracellular structure and function and at the level of international human relations. There is today impressive evidence that the psychological influence of one individual upon another or upon a group is exerted through physiological and biochemical processes, and that the whole organism is involved in all interactions among

9

people. Medicine is concerned with man as a social as well as a biological organism.

With the vast amount of knowledge of man's biological nature revealed by research in the past half century, and the application of that knowledge to protection of man's health, human life expectancy has been increased by more than eighteen years and the material conditions of life have immeasurably improved. But the social environment in which he lives is torn by conflicts that frustrate the human being of today and seriously impede his progress. Clashes occur among individuals and groups; antisocial behavior of adults and adolescents increases alarmingly.

The development of dynamic psychiatry, with the recognition of the role of unconscious motivation in behavior, has brought new understanding and possibility of prediction to the study of man's social nature. It is now demonstrated that the insights that illuminate psychosomatic problems in the individual also throw light on the genesis of social tension. Overt social conflicts are actually symptoms of underlying causes. Direct attack on such symptoms in society as in the individual has proved to be inadequate. Psychiatry is now teaching us to probe into social conflicts for hidden causes. Tension and hostility are often signs of anxiety and insecurity, for when a social structure is threatened, its members and especially its leaders are likely to react to their own anxiety either with appeasement or with aggressive and restrictive measures. The insights and methods of psychiatry, psychology, and cultural anthropology are throwing new light on the emotional disturbances of our world.

Viewing the Macy Foundation's selection of subject areas in which to support research, one discerns intertwining relationships. For example, research and conference discussions on problems of aging include not only the specific areas of arteriosclerosis and other diseases of the circulatory system, but others, such as nutrition, endocrine physiology and pathology, and mental health problems, in which the Foundation has supported research from other points of view. The area of growth and development begins with studies of pregnancy, embryo development, and includes development of personality, endocrinology, nutrition, and other lines of research. Studies of liver function cannot be dissociated from studies of the kidney, the adrenal and other endocrine glands, and of the circulatory system. Physiology of bone is a part of the field of metabolic interrelations. In making their decisions about projects to be assisted the Foundation Directors bear in mind the desirability of encouraging studies that support or extend work being done under other grants. Occasionally the Foundation resumes support of a project once aided but later sponsored by another agency if the research involved has special relevance to other Foundation projects. In this description of the Foundation's activities we hope the reader will see certain fairly well defined lines of development.

With new data, methods, and insights derived from scientific investigation constantly increasing the store of knowledge basic to individual and community health care, the concept of health grows ever broader. It already embraces every level of organization from enzyme systems within the cell to the whole person as a member of his family and social group. Medicine as an art and science, to meet its growing responsibilities, must function in ever more intimate partnership with the physical, biological, and social sciences. A foundation devoted to the advancement and integration of knowledge essential to health care is faced with a challenge of the first magnitude.

WILLARD C. RAPPLEYE
*President*

# THE CONFERENCE PROGRAM

FOUNDATION executives, in their unremitting search for the men and institutions through whom to carry out the foundation's purposes, find two methods of establishing contact with scientists useful: the conversation, usually at infrequent intervals, with an investigator; and the conference attended by a number of persons interested in a certain subject. Each has its advantages and limitations. The Macy Foundation tries to make full use of both.

In its early years the Foundation held conferences as part of its exploring and planning operations. In the summer of 1931, for example, it called a three-day conference of representatives of some twenty-five schools of social work to meet at Bar Harbor, Maine, to examine the needs and possible program of the American Association of Schools of Social Work. The country's economic plight at the time was making new demands upon professional social workers, and the Foundation was assisting a study of the educational needs in the field. Three years later the Foundation organized a four-day meeting, also at Bar Harbor, for a committee of the American Council on Education concerned with the relations of emotions to the educative process. The chairman of the conference was Professor Daniel A. Prescott, who was directing a study of the subject with Foundation support.* At both these conferences prepared papers were read and discussed in the usual manner of scientific meetings.

Another conference that the Foundation held at Bar Harbor, in July, 1936, was something of a departure from the conventional pattern. The participants were a small group of men and women with training and experience in several branches

---

* Prescott. Daniel A , *Emotion and the Educative Process*, American Council on Education, Washington, 1938.

of the medical and social sciences and a common interest in human relations. Each morning and afternoon session of the four-day meeting was presided over by a different chairman. In completely informal round-table discussions, the group talked about clinical approaches to human relations problems. Without laying claim to solutions, they found the experience of sharing thoughts and working through problems together so helpful that they hoped to repeat it, with the inclusion of consultants and investigators from other fields.

In December, 1936, the Foundation provided the repetition, with a four-day conference at the Institute of Human Relations of Yale University. The subject was the study of human relations in the family. A number of those who had attended the Bar Harbor conference were among the thirty family consultants, teachers, sociologists, and representatives of other professions in the group. Again there were no formal presentations or reports, only informal discussion. The object of the meeting was not to answer questions, but to elucidate them. Sharp divergences of opinion about techniques, approaches, and even goals came to the surface, were expressed, some resolved and others not. The multidiscipline conference meeting for several days to discuss informally a topic of common interest had proved itself to the Foundation officers as a promising method for bringing the resources of several professions to focus upon a single problem.

In the summer of 1937, the Foundation brought together in a two-day conference at Falmouth, Massachusetts, a group of scientists interested in problems of aging. The purpose was to assist a project that had been receiving Foundation support for more than a year: the preparation of a volume — a symposium — on aging under the editorship of Dr. E. V. Cowdry.* Under the auspices of the National Research Council and the Union of American Biological Societies, and under the chairmanship of Dr. Cowdry, fifteen of the contributors to the

---

* Cowdry, Edmund V., ed., *Problems of Ageing, Biological and Medical Aspects*, The Williams & Wilkins Company, Baltimore, 1939.

volume and others interested in the processes of aging in plant, animal, and human life, in the clinical, social, and psychological aspects of these processes in human beings, met to combine their data and points of view, so that the volume might be an integrated work. Three years later, in January, 1940, the American division of the International Club for Research on Aging* held its first meeting in Washington, with Foundation support. Many of those who had attended the Falmouth conference were present. The club met annually from that date to 1953. Its name was changed in 1949 to Conference on Problems of Aging.

During the late 1930's and early 1940's, the Foundation arranged and supported a number of conferences devoted to various purposes, some of only one session, others lasting two or more days; some of informal nature, and others following the conventional program of papers read on selected topics and prepared discussion.

In the war years the need for private support of conferences to assist military and civilian organizations engaged in the country's services was great. Many scientists working on related problems or on different aspects of a single problem found themselves isolated by war-time conditions from normal contact with colleagues and free flow of scientific knowledge. The urgent demands of national defense increased the need of investigators to share ideas and data during the course of research instead of relying upon published reports, frequently long delayed.

On its own initiative and at the request of scientists and committees concerned with problems of vital interest to the military services, the Foundation arranged a number of conferences to bring about interchange of experience among investigators in government agencies, universities, hospitals, and commercial laboratories concerned with the same problem. At first participants were both eager and reluctant to share

* *Twentieth Anniversary Review of the Josiah Macy, Jr. Foundation,* New York, 1950, 33-34.

15

their work. The habit of withholding information about research until it is ready for publication is strongly ingrained in many scientists. But in a remarkably short time the common purpose of serving the nation in its peril overcame all other considerations. Investigators exchanged data and plans with complete freedom.

Groups who had found their sessions particularly helpful wished to meet again, and the Foundation arranged for succeeding conferences of the same investigators to continue their discussions. In this way, groups became organizations, and the Foundation's conference program came into being, with more and more groups of scientists asking for sponsorship of multiprofessional conferences to deal with pressing problems. Four groups, those concerned with adrenal cortex, liver injury, bone and wound healing, and shock, had their origins in the wartime meetings.

As more groups were formed, the Foundation officers became more strongly convinced of the usefulness of this technique in the furtherance of research. By the late 1940's, the conference program had become an important part of the Foundation's activity. Groups met from one to three times a year for a period of about three years. The members quickly established friendships that extended beyond the conference table into their professional lives. They learned to accept and interpret data derived from disciplines other than their own, to the advantage of their own investigations. Frequently as a result of exchange of views and results in conferences, members of university or hospital staffs in widely separated cities and of different disciplines planned and carried through joint studies of special problems, bringing together scientific resources not available in any one laboratory.

The Foundation officers selected conference topics from among many suggested, with regard for timeliness of the subject in relation to a specific need, desirability of stimulating research in a hitherto neglected area, apparent need for inter-discipline approach to a problem, relation of the subject to a

16

special scientific interest of the Foundation. Often a subject chosen was one in which the Foundation was supporting research; in these cases the grantees closely concerned were invited to participate.

In 1948, the Foundation Directors signalled their recognition of the importance of the conference program by establishing a separate annual budget and a separate staff for it.

The conference plan, evolved through experience and after discussion with chairmen of several groups, had by that time taken on its present character. Its chief purpose is to bring about communication among scientists. As the accumulation of new knowledge in every branch of science makes specialization ever more necessary, the interdependence of the scientific branches increases. For example, the highly specialized science of nuclear physics has important relations with medical research today because of the tracer techniques and the need for protection against radiation injury. But medicine is also a social science, concerned with man as a social as well as a physiological creature; hence, it includes economic and other social problems in its province.

The multidiscipline approach to research is not widely provided for by our universities, scientific societies, and journals. Further hindrances to it are of semantic and psychological nature. Emotional barriers as well as misunderstanding of terminology frequently interpose themselves between members of related professions in the consideration of a common problem. Spontaneous, untrammelled discussion in a small group and an atmosphere of "free-floating security" breaks down barriers insurmountable by conventional methods of communication.

The Macy Foundation conferences avoid the pattern of presentation of finished research followed by formal, planned discussion. Interchange of opinion and data while an investigation is in progress is the aim, rather than presentation or defense of conclusions. In preparation for the conference, the chairman, usually in consultation with Foundation officers, selects a phase of the general subject for discussion at each session, and asks a member of the group or a guest who may have pertinent experience to introduce the topic. At the first session, it is made clear that the group is free to make any desired changes in method of conducting the meetings. No part of the structure is rigid. The introductory remarks may be fairly long reports of current work, or brief, provocative statements of views. They are never formal presentations such as are delivered at the usual scientific convention. The speaker may ask to be allowed to proceed without interruption until he has finished his essential matter; unless he does, discussion will begin almost at once, with interjection of questions, corroboration, or challenge, and continue at lively pace throughout the session. Participants are encouraged to come prepared with any material that may be germane to the topic. Pockets may be bulging with slides, diagrams, notes — anything that may prove useful.

Each group consists of a nucleus of some fifteen continuing members selected by the chairman in consultation with the Macy Foundation. Representatives of as many pertinent disciplines as possible are chosen, each one an investigator who has made significant contribution to the group's subject. New members are added from time to time to fill gaps in point of view or technique, and guests are invited to each meeting. The total number attending a conference is usually limited to twenty-five to make possible the fullest participation by every one. Since 1951, the Foundation has arranged for at least one guest from abroad and has made it possible for him to visit clinics and laboratories while he is in the United States.

Length of the term through which a conference group would last varied considerably in the early years. Some groups, at the end of the period originally agreed upon, were reorganized with some of the former members and new ones from other disciplines to change the direction and emphasis of the discussions. This policy was found unsatisfactory for various reasons. Finally a five-year duration for all groups was decided upon and has been adhered to ever since, even though often with great reluctance on the part of the Foundation to see a group disbanded.

The longest record of any conference group, with virtually the same membership from its inception in 1940 to January, 1953, is that of the Conference on Problems of Aging. Nine charter members of the Club for Research on Aging were still members of the group in 1953. Most of the other members active at its termination joined the group in the early 1940's.

The war-born group on Bone and Wound Healing, concerned originally with treatment to accelerate the healing of fractures, almost at once expanded its area to include wound healing in general. Within a year it changed its designation to Metabolic Aspects of Convalescence Including Bone and Wound Healing, reflecting the wider scope its inquiries had taken. Later "Bone and Wound Healing" disappeared from the title. The group held its seventeenth and final meeting in March, 1948. A year later a new group with many of the same members as the earlier one held its first meeting under the title of Metabolic Interrelations; its fifth and final meeting occurred in January, 1953.

Conference groups now meet once a year, with an occasional exception. In the first years of the program some met several times a year, especially some of the war-time groups.

In the first years of the program each conference lasted for two days, with morning, afternoon, and evening sessions on the first day, morning and afternoon sessions on the second. Soon it was observed that the informal dinner preceding the evening session of the first day was remarkably effective in establishing easy communication among conferees. To make the fullest use of this stimulating occasion, the conference plan was altered in 1952 to open with a dinner and a session on the evening before the first full day and usually to leave the second evening free for small group discussions. At the opening session members and guests are asked to introduce themselves with enough information about their professional training and experience to account for their interest in the subject of the conference. A regular feature of Macy Foundation conferences — of the special ones as well as of those in the continuing program — is the morning and afternoon mid-session break for refreshments. It is the one item on the agenda that may be said to be enforced, for its beneficial effects are invaluable.

In 1942, the Macy Foundation held a two-day conference on Cerebral Inhibition. The twenty participants included representatives of anthropology, psychobiology, physiology, psychiatry, neurology, psychology, medicine, anatomy, and electronics. They shared an interest in the physiological mechanisms underlying the phenomena of conditioned reflexes and hypnosis as related to the problem of cerebral inhibition. A year later an essay on the teleological aspects of behavior* was published by a physiologist who had attended the conference and two mathematicians who had not. It aroused interest in study of the mechanisms of behavior, particularly the so-called feedback mechanisms that control or affect behavior. The concept of the feedback mechanism was borrowed by students of human behavior from workers in the physical sciences, notably electronics engineering. For example, in the early days of radio, engineers discovered that the volume of reception could be increased by feeding back into the receiver some of the first stages of amplification. The concept is applicable to study of biological and social behavior — in fact, to understanding of many aspects of man's activity.

Attracted by the prospect of wide-ranging multidiscipline co-operation, a number of those who had participated in the 1942 meeting sought to carry the effort further. In March, 1946, the Macy Foundation organized a conference group devoted to feedback mechanisms in biology and the social sciences. Besides two regular conferences in the first year, the group participated in special meetings on teleological mechanisms. With the holding of the sixth conference in 1949, the

---

* Rosenbleuth, Arturo; Wiener, Norbert; and Bigelow, Julian, "Behavior, Purpose and Teleology," *Philosophy of Science*, 1943, *10*, 18.

group adopted as its name the title of Norbert Wiener's provocative book published the year before* — Cybernetics — adding as a subtitle Circular Causal and Feedback Mechanisms in Biological and Social Systems.

The Cybernetics group, which held its last conference in 1953, included seven of the participants in the 1942 conference. The continuing members represented the fields of electrical engineering, mathematics, sociology, anthropology, psychology, psychiatry, biology, physiology, anatomy, zoology. Still other disciplines were represented by guests. It was the most widely diverse of the Foundation's conference groups, with, therefore, the most challenging problems of communication to solve. Its lively sessions afforded a rich experience in bringing the insights and techniques of many divisions of scientific knowledge to bear on topics of fundamental import to all, demonstrating anew the essential unity of science, no matter how specialized its branches have or may become.

At the earliest of the Foundation conferences, notes of the discussions were taken, summarized, mimeographed or otherwise reproduced, and distributed to the members of the group. The conferences held during the war were recorded more fully by expert reporters, edited by the Foundation and one or more members of the groups, and the proceedings, in brief form at first, more expanded for later sessions, were privately printed by the Foundation as paper-bound pamphlets and distributed to the members of the group and to selected military and other governmental agencies within the United States and abroad through the facilities of the war-time reprint service.

As conference followed conference and new groups came into existence, interest in the transactions spread beyond the circle of members. Many who had received the war-time reports had found them useful, as had colleagues who came upon them in laboratories and libraries. During 1946-1949, the Foundation prepared fuller reports of the conferences,

---

* Wiener, Norbert, *Cybernetics*, John Wiley & Sons, New York, 1948.

21

published them in pamphlet form, usually by photo-offset process, and sold them at less than cost. The transactions rapidly became an important part of the conference program. Since 1950, they have been published by letterpress in hard covers with jackets. Demand for them has grown until, in 1954, 13,748 copies were sold, approximately a fourth of them outside the United States.

The difficulties attending preparation of reports of such informal meetings as the Macy Foundation conferences are formidable. There is first the impossibility of transmitting via the printed page the personal contact that takes place around the conference table. The spoken words are often lifeless without the eloquent raising of an eyebrow or ironic smile that accompanied them; perhaps their meaning is quite lost without the speaker's tone of voice or flash of eye as he said them. One can only make the most careful selections possible of the telling phrase, hoping that the reader may sense the interactions among the group members that produced and followed the words. Though illustrative material is published, it is not possible to present all the matter shown to the members, some of it in very unfinished form. Repetitions and irrelevancies can be removed to an extent; but if the interest in smooth flow and unity of subject matter is pursued exclusively, there may be sacrifice of spontaneity and other essential characteristics of the uninhibited process which it is the purpose of the conferences to encourage. In the deletions made by the participants from the verbatim stenotype-recorded transcripts and those made by the group's editor, it is inevitable that a question or remark needed to clarify a subsequent statement will be removed. Even the unedited transcripts contain questions asked and never answered, points raised and never settled. If sessions continued around the clock for many days, not all the questions arising among groups of such inquiring minds would be neatly wrapped up. Interruptions, deviations, disagreements not only occur; they are encouraged. When disagreements persist, every effort is made to mobilize the resources of the group in order to specify the nature of the disagreement and to outline the new research necessary to resolve the issue. Frequently the problem is cleared up by discovery that the investigators had used different methods of measurement or different experimental animals, or had rested their arguments upon contradictory basic assumptions. Gaps in knowledge, failure in technique, limitations as well as potentialities in work done and contemplated are brought to light, for their revelation may — often does — lead to progress by someone else if not by the original investigator.

The transactions, never intended as logically developed treatises of a given subject, take the reader into a small, intimate gathering of scientists, letting him hear an exchange of ideas, data, hypotheses tested and to be tested, as experts think out loud, individually and collectively, about their work — precisely the kind of matter excluded from traditional scientific publications. Members of conference groups and European guests have reported that students read the transactions avidly and apparently with profit.

Though the publication of the transactions is of secondary importance to the work of the conferences, the volumes do extend in some degree the influence of the conferences. The nine groups now active number among their regular members more than two hundred scientists from more than a hundred universities, hospitals, research institutions, and government agencies. A far greater representation could be counted among the memberships of groups that have completed their terms. Most of the participants are investigators, teachers, deans, and administrators with responsibility for the expenditure of large sums for research and education. The topics they discuss include or touch upon many of the subject areas in which the national government annually spends millions of dollars for research. Therefore, through direct contact and publication, the stimulus of the conference program reaches out in ever widening circles. Aware of this fact, and repeatedly assured by participants of the usefulness of the unstructured meeting devoted to an important subject, the Directors of the Macy Foundation are confident that the conference program is an experiment in communication among scientists and in the integration of scientific knowledge well worth continuing.

## MACY FOUNDATION CONFERENCE GROUPS

| Topics | Chairmen | Dates |
|---|---|---|
| ADMINISTRATIVE MEDICINE | DR. HUGH R. LEAVELL | 1953- |
| ADRENAL CORTEX | DR. C. N. H. LONG | 1949-1953 |
| BIOLOGICAL ANTIOXIDANTS | DR. PAUL GYÖRGY | 1946-1950 |
| BLOOD CLOTTING AND ALLIED PROBLEMS | DR. IRVING S. WRIGHT | 1948-1952 |
| COLD INJURY | DR. JOHN H. TALBOTT | 1951- |
| CONNECTIVE TISSUES | DR. W. PAUL HOLBROOK | 1950-1954 |
| CYBERNETICS (originally Circular Causal and Feedback Mechanisms in Biological and Social Systems) | DR. WARREN S. McCULLOCH | 1946-1953 |
| FACTORS REGULATING BLOOD PRESSURE | DR. HARRY GOLDBLATT | 1947-1951 |
| GESTATION | DR. GEORGE WISLOCKI | 1954- |
| GROUP PROCESSES | DR. HOWARD S. LIDDELL | 1954- |

| | | |
|---|---|---|
| LIVER INJURY | DR. CECIL J. WATSON<br>DR. CHARLES H. BEST | 1943-1953 |
| METABOLIC INTERRELATIONS<br>(originally Bone and Wound<br>Healing, then Metabolic<br>Aspects of Convalescence) | DR. FULLER ALBRIGHT<br>DR. WALLACE D. ARMSTRONG | 1942-1953 |
| NERVE IMPULSE | DR. H. HOUSTON MERRITT | 1950-1954 |
| NEUROPHARMACOLOGY | DR. HUDSON HOAGLAND | 1954- |
| PROBLEMS OF AGING<br>(originally Club for Re-<br>search on Aging) | DR. WILLIAM DE B. MACNIDER<br>DR. EDMUND V. COWDRY<br>DR. ROY G. HOSKINS | 1940-1953 |
| PROBLEMS OF CONSCIOUSNESS | DR. DAVID G. WRIGHT<br>DR. ROY R. GRINKER | 1950-1954 |
| PROBLEMS OF INFANCY AND<br>CHILDHOOD<br>(originally Problems of<br>Early Infancy) | DR. LEO BARTEMEIER | 1947-1953 |
| RENAL FUNCTION | DR. ROBERT F. PITTS | 1949-1953 |
| SHOCK AND CIRCULATORY<br>HOMEOSTASIS | DR. EPHRAIM SHORR | 1951- |

25

# NATIONAL DEFENSE

IN THE FALL of 1940, the Directors of the Foundation, fore-
seeing the eventual involvement of the United States in war,
began to support projects that would have special bearing
upon the nation's health and problems of defense. During the
next five years the Foundation spent more than $630,000 in
aid of undertakings in medical research and education with
direct relation to the war. More than sixty percent of all the
money appropriated in 1941-1945 was used for these purposes.

Two subject areas of importance to war-time problems were
part of earlier Foundation interests: traumatic shock, closely
related to surgical shock, and war neurosis, a phase of the
psychosomatic interrelations in which the Foundation had
encouraged studies since 1931. Reviews of the literature in
these two areas were begun at once.

## Traumatic Shock

The reaction known as "traumatic shock," characterized by
a progressive lowering of blood pressure often not reversible
by transfusion or circulatory stimulants, had been investigated
by two of the world's leading physiologists, Dr. Walter B.
Cannon of Harvard University and Sir William Bayliss of
Oxford, in the war of 1914-1918. Dr. Cannon's conclusion was
that in cases of combat injury a toxic substance entered the
blood stream and caused dilation of the small blood vessels
with resulting fall in pressure. Neither Dr. Cannon during
the war nor other investigators subsequently were able to
identify the substance or even to prove its existence. In post-
war research and practice, traumatic shock following injuries
sustained in civilian life was generally recognized as similar
to surgical shock following operations involving prolonged
anesthesia or unusual loss of blood.

27

By 1940, two investigators in New York University's Department of Biology, Dr. Robert Chambers and Dr. Benjamin W. Zweifach, whose work on capillary permeability had been supported by the Foundation, had produced a most significant observation. They noted that epinephrine accentuates the rate and degree of rhythmic narrowing of the smallest arteries leading into the capillary network — a process which regulates the blood flow to the tissues. Then they found that injury to a frog causing loss of blood at first increased, but later decreased, the response to epinephrine. In this second phase blood flowed into the dilated capillaries and became stagnant. A progressive fall in blood pressure ensued, and when the condition had become established, no transfusions or other treatment could prevent the death of the frog. The two men made similar observations on rats. The reaction resembled traumatic shock in man.

Through a series of monthly conferences on traumatic shock arranged by the Foundation, Dr. Chambers came into collaboration with Dr. Magnus I. Gregersen, chairman of the group and Professor of Physiology at the College of Physicians and Surgeons, Columbia University, whose research on traumatic shock the Foundation was supporting.* When Dr. Chambers injected into rats samples of blood from dogs suffering from experimentally-induced traumatic shock, which Dr. Gregersen furnished, the result was a shock-like response in the blood vessels of the rats. The fact appeared to confirm Dr. Cannon's hypothesis about a toxic substance in blood produced by injury and causing traumatic shock.

During the summer of 1943, another collaboration was brought about by a series of Foundation conferences — the group concerned with physiology and pathology of the liver. Dr. Paul György, then Assistant Professor of Pediatrics at Western Reserve University School of Medicine, who was re-

---

* After United States entry into the war, the studies became a defense project under the auspices of the National Research Council. The Foundation supported the investigation from 1940 to 1945.

ceiving Foundation support for studies of the influence of nutrition on louse infestation in rats and man, reported at a conference that he had been unable to make serial studies of the progress of cirrhosis of the liver induced in rats by a diet deficient in certain substances because the rats died after the minor operation made to obtain fragments of liver. This fact was surprising, because rats are hardy creatures and usually recover after removal of as much as half of the liver.

Another member of the conference was Dr. Ephraim Shorr, Associate Professor of Medicine at Cornell University Medical College and also a member of the conference on traumatic shock. Dr. Shorr was thoroughly familiar with the work of Dr. Chambers and Dr. Zweifach and its bearing on the earlier theory of Dr. Cannon. He conceived the idea that the cause of death of Dr. György's rats was traumatic shock, and that the source of the toxic substance suggested by Dr. Cannon and demonstrated by Dr. Chambers and his associates might be the livers of the animals damaged by diet deficiency. The Foundation later supported a study of this possibility by Dr. Shorr. An early result of the new study was the identification of ferritin, an iron-containing protein produced by the liver, as the toxic substance discovered by Dr. Chambers and Dr. Zweifach. Dr. Shorr was able to show that when the liver suffers from lack of oxygen or from malnutrition, ferritin is released into the blood stream and blocks the regulating action of epinephrine upon the capillary blood flow and thereby induces traumatic shock.*

Thus two Macy Foundation conferences concerned with problems of vital importance to the war effort brought about co-operation between the laboratories of Dr. Chambers and Dr. Gregersen, enabled Dr. Shorr to learn of Dr. György's experience with rats suffering from experimental cirrhosis of the liver, and led to the important work of Dr. Shorr (joined by Dr. Zweifach) at the Cornell University Medical College,

* See pages 130-132 for an account of Dr. Shorr's research.

a project still being carried on by Dr. Shorr, with Foundation support, and making valuable contributions to medical knowledge.

The Foundation made war-time grants to assist studies of traumatic shock also at Harvard Medical School's Department of Surgery, at the Massachusetts General Hospital, at the Department of Radiology of the University of Rochester School of Medicine and Dentistry, the Department of Physiology of the Johns Hopkins University School of Medicine, the Department of Medicine at the University of Minnesota Medical School, the Bowman Gray School of Medicine of Wake Forest College, the Department of Surgery at Vanderbilt University School of Medicine, and the Department of Physiology of the Yale University School of Medicine.

## Army Air Force Rheumatic Fever Control Program

An inevitable accompaniment of war is the high incidence of infectious diseases, particularly of the respiratory tract, as troops are suddenly brought to mobilization centers and put into contact with men from distant regions, exposed to infections for which they have little or no resistance because of having had no previous exposure. Streptococcus infections and rheumatic fever were especially troublesome in the last great war.

Rheumatic fever quickly became epidemic at several Army Air Force installations, threatening the possibility of a nation-wide epidemic. The Air Surgeon, Major General David N. Grant, authorized an extensive study of the problem. Through contact with Colonel William Paul Holbrook, Chief of the Professional Services, Office of the Air Surgeon, Foundation officers learned that assistance was needed in co-ordinating the research being conducted at widely separated hospitals and camps and in providing specialized laboratory training for medical officers and funds for equipment.

The Foundation, therefore, made a grant to Columbia University, College of Physicians and Surgeons, to support a study

30

of the epidemiology of rheumatic fever and streptococcus infections in a military setting. Dr. Alexander B. Gutman, Assistant Professor of Medicine, undertook direction of the project. Some twenty medical and laboratory Army Air Force officers were temporarily assigned to him for intensive training in identification and typing of various forms of streptococci. The training was given at the College of Physicians and Surgeons and at the Rockefeller Institute for Medical Research. The officers returned to their stations provided with the special knowledge and equipment for typing streptococci. The procedures they introduced, incorporated into the Army Air Forces' medical program, insured a uniform method of assembling and analyzing data from widely separted Air Force bases.

The Air Surgeon, in co-operation with the Foundation, issued a special monthly bulletin called *The Army Air Forces Rheumatic Fever News Letter* which, from August, 1944, through October, 1945, was distributed by the Foundation's reprint service to medical officers of the Air Force, to medical installations of the Army and Navy, and to selected medical libraries in this country and abroad. It kept widely distant medical officers in touch with all the progress being made in the control and treatment of rheumatic fever.

The Foundation's grant to Columbia included support for a survey of the incidence of various forms of streptococci in the noses and throats of large groups of people and for a study by the Office of the Air Surgeon of streptococcus sore throat, meningococcus meningitis, and other infectious diseases. Sulfadiazine given in small doses to several thousand men in camps was found to give considerable protection against a number of these infections. Later all three branches of the military service extensively adopted the sulfadiazine preventive treatment.

### Chemotherapeutic Aerosols

An early concern of military medical authorities was the possibility that the enemy might use poison gas. In addition to the immediate casualties occurring in a gas attack, there are likely to be many more from secondary infections — pneumonia, bronchitis, and the like — because inhaling the gases would have much the same effect upon the surface of the mucous membrane that an attack of influenza has: an impairment of natural protection against infection. Pneumococci and streptococci that are normal inhabitants of the respiratory tract are harmless as long as the mucous membrane lining of the tract remains healthy.

In the summer of 1942, Foundation officers learned from conversations with representatives of the Technical Division of the Chemical Warfare Service that they needed help in finding methods for protection of the respiratory tract and the lungs against the secondary infection likely to follow the injurious effects of gas inhalation.

At this point a project previously supported by the Foundation became pertinent. Lt. Col. Harold A. Abramson (then Major) of the Office of the Chief, Technical Division, Chemical Warfare Service, for some time before his appointment as a medical officer, had been conducting research on allergy, with Foundation assistance, at the College of Physicians and Surgeons and at Mt. Sinai Hospital. He had developed an efficient method of controlling the size of aerosol droplets, a method making it possible to use an aerosol mist with minute droplets capable of passing through the smallest bronchial tubes into the depths of the lungs or larger droplets that would lodge in the trachea or bronchi. He was selected to direct a research project at the Long Island Biological Laboratories, Cold Spring Harbor, supported jointly by the Foundation and the War Department, to produce an aerosol for prevention of respiratory infection.

Lt. Col. Abramson began with a solution of sodium hypochlorite (the photographer's "hypo" solution) which the British had used in their air raid shelters. A mist generated by steam could be sprayed into barracks to destroy the bacteria in the atmosphere. The Office of the Air Surgeon arranged for a barrack at Mitchell Field to be used for tests. Men suffered no discomfort from sleeping in air saturated with sodium hypochlorite, but their rifles and other metal equipment were corroded. The solution therefore had to be abandoned for use in military posts.

At that time penicillin was amazing scientists and laymen with its therapeutic value. At the suggestion of Foundation officers, Lt. Col. Abramson authorized the experimental use of a penicillin aerosol with animals. It was found that the drug was absorbed by the lungs. An investigator at the Long Island Biological Laboratory, Dr. Vernon Bryson, volunteered to test the inhalation on himself, and found that it entered the lungs without causing any damage. The Foundation supported further research at the Long Island Laboratories to produce a penicillin aerosol suitable for human use.

Then collaboration between the Technical Division of the Chemical Warfare Service, the Long Island Biological Laboratories, and the Department of Medicine, College of Physicians and Surgeons, Columbia University, was begun in 1944 with another grant from the Foundation. Dr. Alvan L. Barach undertook a clinical program that soon proved the protective efficacy of inhalations of penicillin aerosols against otherwise fatal streptococcus infections of animals and against infections of the lungs and upper respiratory tract of men. It was found also that enough penicillin was absorbed from the inhaled aerosol to be carried in high concentration through the blood stream.

On the basis of this study, the Surgeon General arranged the standardization of nebulizers to be used by medical officers for aerosol inhalation therapy. Fortunately, there was no occasion to find out whether the method would protect troops against the secondary infections following gas poisoning, but inhalation of penicillin in fine droplets has become a widely used practice in this country and Great Britain. It is one of the simplest means of using the antibiotic in home treatment of infections of the respiratory tract, the lungs, and even for sinusitis. Dr. Barach continued his research into the clinical uses of the aerosol for some time, with Foundation support lasting into 1951.

## Bone and Wound Healing; Convalescence

Investigators were much occupied with work on problems of calcification and bone metabolism early in the war for their importance in treating fractures and other wounds. At the request of the Committee on Clinical Investigation of the National Research Council, Dr. Fuller Albright, Associate Professor of Medicine at the Harvard Medical School, organized a discussion group of some thirty members representing ten universities and research institutions in the United States and Canada to deal with bone and wound healing. Medical officers of the United States, Canada, and France attended some of its meetings. In 1943 the group widened its field to include metabolic aspects of convalescence; its discussions clarified many puzzling questions about protein deficiency following operation or injury. Published transactions of the group's meetings were of notable assistance to the armed services of our country and those of our allies. Supported from its beginning by the Foundation, the group became a part of the continuing conference program.*

Dr. Albright at Harvard Medical School made important studies of the influence of nutrition and hormones, especially those of the adrenal cortex, in the building up of protein supplies in the body. The Foundation contributed to support of his research for the three years 1943-1945. During the same period the Foundation aided a study of the influence of nutrition upon fracture healing and disuse atrophy of bone by Dr. W. D. Armstrong at the Department of Physiology at the University of Minnesota Medical School. Dr. Charles D. Kochakian, Associate in Physiology in the Department of Vital Economics, University of Rochester, School of Medicine and Dentistry, who had been making studies of the physiology

---

* See page 19.

34

of androgens, found that they could be used to hasten wound healing. With Foundation support from 1942 through 1945, he made extensive studies of their influence on bone and wound healing.

A pioneering project that brought new and valuable knowledge to the treatment of wounds was that of Mrs. Ruth S. Hoffman, a biologist who, while working in Palestine, found that an extract of heart muscle would accelerate tissue growth in the test tube. Clinical tests made on wounded soldiers in British Army hospitals showed that the material, when applied directly to wounds, promoted the healing process. With the co-operation of Dr. William DeW. Andrus, of the Department of Surgery, Cornell University Medical College, and with a small grant from the Foundation, Mrs. Hoffman was able to confirm her findings by animal experiments. A two-year research project conducted at Cornell Medical College in 1944-1946 carried her work into clinical application.

### War Neurosis

A field in which the Foundation undertook assistance to the government in anticipation of the inevitable entry of the nation into war was that of military psychiatric problems. In the fall of 1940, it gave funds to the National Research Council for the first meeting of the Committee on Neuropsychiatry and distributed to the members of the committee and to the liaison officers from the armed services and Selective Service copies of a report on acute war neuroses suffered by troops removed from Dunkirk.* The National Research Council appointed a sub-committee to co-operate with Selective Service and the armed forces on the subject of war neuroses.

Selective Service immediately found that there were not enough psychiatrists available for individual examination of men. The only possibility was a procedure for personality testing that could be administered to groups simultaneously. As a first step toward working out such procedures the Founda-

---

* Sargant, W., and Slater, E., "Acute War Neuroses," *Lancet*, 1940, 2, 1.

tion sponsored a two-day conference in Philadelphia bringing psychiatrists and psychologists together with representatives of the armed forces and Selective Service for discussion of the problem. Out of this conference developed a series of projects under the auspices of the National Research Council and assisted by the Foundation at Columbia University, Cornell University, Harvard University, the Menninger Foundation, and the University of Wisconsin. Four new group screening procedures came from these projects, were carefully developed and widely used by Selective Service and the armed forces.*

As the conflict brought ever more individuals into situations of stress and war neuroses became an increasingly serious problem, the Foundation sponsored a number of critical reviews of the literature and distributed them to medical officers through its reprint service.

Screening processes, however revealing they might be when carefully applied, were insufficient to help in the reduction of war neuroses, as experience soon proved. The problem was much more complex than mere detection of nervous disorders or severe personality difficulties. Men whom an individual examination would have eliminated from the forces slipped through the tests and some of them adjusted successfully to later experiences, including prolonged combat duty. Others who gave every indication of normal mental health and who served heroically on the field broke in the face of an apparently minor occurrence. Causes of breakdown could not be easily classified; there were too many factors involved, such as nature and duration of stress, the man's personal history, his relationship with wife or family, his emotional make-up and motivation, the morale of his group, and the quality of leadership under which he served. Malnutrition and infection also affected

---

* The Shipley personality test, by Walter C Shipley under the auspices of the National Research Council, the group Rorschach test and the multiple choice Rorschach test developed by Dr. Molly R. Harrower at the University of Wisconsin; and the Cornell selectee index by Dr. Harold G. Wolff and his associates at Cornell University Medical College. All four tests have been described in monographs and other publications

behavior. Psychiatrists in the military service and from civilian life made continuous efforts, which the Foundation assisted at every opportunity, to bring to our military leaders the understanding that a high incidence of nervous breakdown in a unit was more often traceable to inadequate leadership of officers than to cowardice or lack of character of the men.

Among undertakings assisted by the Foundation for the improvement of psychiatric war services were: two conferences of New York psychiatrists in the spring of 1942 called at the suggestion of Dr. Daniel Blain, Surgeon (R) of the United States Public Health Service, Medical Director of the Recruitment and Manning Organization of the War Shipping Administration, to consider the problems of Merchant Marine personnel, who were subjected to great war dangers; a national conference at the New York Academy of Medicine in January, 1943, sponsored by the Foundation jointly with the United States Public Health Service, at which medical representatives of our armed forces, the Public Health Service, the Veterans Administration, and other war agencies as well as representatives of the armed services of Canada, Great Britain, and Norway, met with civilian psychiatrists; the editing, reproducing, and distribution to medical officers of the monograph *War Neuroses in North Africa* by Lt. Col. Roy R. Grinker and Major John P. Spiegel,* a treatise which the Air Surgeon considered a milestone in the progress of understanding and treatment of that disability; publication and distribution of additional monographs for the Office of the Air Surgeon.

Through its efforts to help medical officers inform themselves of new methods of diagnosing and treating mental illness, the Macy Foundation made probably its most important contribution to the war effort, for no other medical problem

---

* When military restrictions were lifted, the monograph, which had been a "restricted" document of the Air Surgeon's Office, was republished for general distribution. Grinker, Lt. Col Roy R. (M.C.), and Spiegel, Major John P. (M.C.), *War Neuroses*, The Blakiston Company, New York, 1945.

37

was so serious. The country was shocked to learn that Selective Service had rejected as unfit for military duty because of nervous and mental disorders 1,840,000 of the fifteen million men examined. In spite of rejections, psychological casualties among our military personnel resulted in a million hospital admissions for psychiatric and psychosomatic breakdown. More than 600,000 members of Army personnel were removed from theatres of operation because of breakdown, a number greater than the total of those wounded in battle action and more than twice the number of men killed in battle. Mental disturbances or personality problems caused the discharge of more than 700,000 men from the armed forces in the course of the war. The problem continues to tax the services of the Veterans Administration, which is still carrying a heavy case load of neuropsychiatric patients from the two wars of 1914-1918 and 1941-1945.

## Other Grants

Projects in various areas of medical service to the armed forces and to civilians engaged in supplying war needs were assisted by Foundation grants. Among them were: a study of human acclimatization to hot environments conducted at the Department of Physiology, College of Physicians and Surgeons, Columbia University, in collaboration with the Army Signal Corps for two years; an investigation of physical and mental fatigue occurring at high altitude made at the Fatigue Laboratory of the Department of Industrial Research, Harvard University Graduate School of Business Administration; studies of the influence of nutrition upon louse infestation in rats and man at the Western Reserve School of Medicine, Department of Pediatrics, and later in the same Department of the University of Pennsylvania School of Medicine; an investigation of brain injuries in war service at the Harvard University Medical School; studies of liver disease in the Schick General Hospital in a collaboration between the University of Minnesota Medical School's Department of Medicine and the Office of the Surgeon

General of the Army; a survey of geographical distribution of tropical diseases in the Pacific and preparation of a manual on the subject made by the Department of Biology of Stanford University.

With the needs of the armed forces draining the nation's supply of medically trained personnel, the problems of medical schools became acute. The Foundation assisted the Association of American Medical Colleges during the war years with grants in aid of conferences and consultations.

A problem always acute in war times is that of treating burns. When the disaster at the Boston night club, the Cocoanut Grove, on November 28, 1942, filled the city's hospitals with casualties from one of the worst fires in our history, the Massachusetts General Hospital staff successfully treated many badly burned patients with intravenous injection of human plasma for shock, simple ointment for local application, sulfadiazine to prevent infection, and surgery for reconstruction. Thinking that the medical branches of the armed services might find an account of the experience useful, the hospital staff, with assistance from the Foundation, published a record of many case histories in book form* and the Foundation distributed some fifteen hundred copies to Army and Navy hospitals. One recipient of the book reported that it had been of great use to him and his fellow officers in the management of fifty-five cases of serious burns resulting from a naval disaster.

After the Cocoanut Grove fire, the Foundation supported an investigation into the treatment of deep burns conducted at the Massachusetts General Hospital under the direction of Dr. Oliver Cope, Assistant Professor of Surgery, Harvard Medical School, with assistance also from the Committee on Medical Research of the Office of Scientific Research and Development and Harvard University.

---

* *Management of the Cocoanut Grove Burns at the Massachusetts General Hospital,* J. B. Lippincott Company, Philadelphia, 1943.

39

JOSIAH MACY JR. FOUNDATION

War Reprint Service

When war takes great numbers of physicians and surgeons from their normal activities, puts them into uniform, and scatters them wherever the military forces are fighting, often presenting them with problems for which their training and practice have given them little or no precedent, their need for contact with medical libraries and university facilities via the printed page becomes acute. In the vast war of 1941-1945 this problem confronted our military doctors just as it had in the Civil War, when for the first time in our history a huge military medical service was called into being in haste and scattered far and wide, with primitive or no means of communication between its members and their colleagues at home. One of the magnificent accomplishments of that band of pioneering humanitarians who formed the United States Sanitary Commission, the forerunner of the American Red Cross, was its preparation and distribution to medical officers of the Union army of papers on epidemic diseases, surgical techniques, hospital management, problems of hygiene and nutrition, etc., written by the country's leading medical experts for the guidance of civilian doctors in a citizen army.

The Macy Foundation attempted to perform something of the same service in the war of 1941-1945. With the help of the Committee on Pathology of the National Research Council and the National Committee for Mental Hygiene, the Foundation selected articles bearing on military medical problems, reproduced them, and sent them to military medical officers far and near. The enterprise was begun as an experiment on a small scale. It met with such enthusiastic response that it was gradually enlarged to meet the demands. The Surgeons General of the Army and Navy and the Air Surgeon cooperated. In the three years 1943-1945, more than five million copies of some four hundred medical and scientific articles were sent to medical officers of our own forces and some of those of the services of Canada, the United Kingdom, New Zealand, Australia, India, and China. Monthly distribution

40

reached more than twenty thousand officers at the height of the service. A million or more reprints were sent to medical officers responsible for care of neuropsychiatric disorders, an operation assisted by the National Committee for Mental Hygiene and Mr. and Mrs. Harry Frank of Kintnersville, Pennsylvania, who lent their home and personal services to the mailing of the reprints.

The reprint service was able to assist two other government agencies as well as the military organizations. In 1945, the Department of State asked the Foundation to send 103,000 copies of selected reprints to 162 United States consulates in fifty countries for the use of civilian physicians. The Office of War Information reproduced a number of the Foundation's publications for its own distribution abroad.

At the termination of the reprint service in 1946, unused reprints were sent to twelve war devastated countries. More than $200,000 had been spent in this three-year service to our fighting forces.

Acknowledgments received from medical personnel in remote places testified eloquently to the usefulness of the material sent out. Many wrote with unmistakable sincerity of their gratitude for the only recent medical literature they had seen since leaving home and of the practical use they had made of the material.

# MEDICAL EDUCATION

THE RAPID ADVANCE of medical education within a comparatively few decades from something little better than a trade apprenticeship to the status of a full university department with standards as high as those of any branch of learning has brought problems to challenge the best of American organizing ability and resources of money and brains. The United States for some time has been more liberally supplied with well-trained physicians than most other nations. Problems of distribution between urban and rural areas and the multiplicity of medical services called into being by wide public recognition of the benefits of modern medical care have increased the demand for physicians and other trained workers. The resulting pressure upon the medical schools poses financial difficulties of considerable gravity. Caught between the need for increasing enrollments and facilities without raising tuition fees beyond their already high level and of maintaining high standards of scientific training, the medical schools have found their resources inadequate.

Changed points of view with respect to the physician's role have brought about a reorientation of emphasis in medical teaching. Along with the growth of medical knowledge and resultant specialization, there has been a movement to restore something of the doctor-patient relationship that existed when the family physician was the sole source of medical service. The trend is visible in modifications of undergraduate curricula looking toward restoring the patient as a person to the center of the stage. Such terms as psychosomatic medicine, environmental medicine, comprehensive medicine, and social medicine label courses designed to serve the purpose of training the student to co-ordinate the physiological, biochemical, socio-economic information about a patient. As a practicing physi-

43

cian, he must be able to determine what laboratory tests are required, what social and economic data are relevant to understanding his patient. He will not obtain this information himself, any more than he will make the chemical examination of the patient's blood. But he must be able to ask for, integrate, and apply the data provided by others.

Recognition of the broader knowledge the physician of today needs has led some educators to recommend the revision of curricula to emphasize social and economic aspects of health problems. These matters, important as they are in achieving the view of the patient in relation to his environment, must supplement, but never be substituted for, adequate training in the basic medical sciences. The primary aim of undergraduate medical education is to give the student a solid foundation for later development, a foundation of systematic scientific knowledge, methods of study, and attitudes of mind that will enable him to continue the life-long process of medical education. For with every passing year it becomes more clear that there can be no pause in the doctor's learning. New knowledge comes to light so rapidly and with such profound effect upon accepted views and methods that much of what a student is taught in medical school becomes modified if not invalidated within a short time.

A problem facing the medical profession of our country today is the regulation of the graduates of foreign medical schools who are entering practice here in large numbers, chiefly via internships and residencies in our hospitals. Many of these graduates have practiced medicine in their own countries, though their preparation may have been in every respect below that required of our own candidates for license to practice. Most foreign schools do not restrict their enrollments to numbers for which their teaching facilities are adequate. Instruction is chiefly didactic, with little provision for bedside teaching, laboratory experience, and other features considered essential in the United States. With a general dearth of interns

44

and residents, a situation aggravated by the demands of our defense forces, many hospitals with little or no educational opportunities accept foreign graduates in these posts and so fail to provide the highest quality of professional care to their patients. In some states, graduates of foreign schools are eligible to take state licensing board examinations after one or two years of internship in an "approved" hospital. This can result in the licensing of many physicians who lack the training in the basic medical sciences that has been the foundation of American medical education for fifty years; it can bring about a serious lowering of our standards of education and practice.

Measures that have been suggested to prevent the ill effects of this situation are: 1) to stimulate the medical boards of the smaller hospitals and municipal institutions to provide a supervised educational experience for recent medical graduates; 2) to revise the policy of approval of hospitals for internships and residencies; 3) to devise an acceptable mechanism for evaluating individually the competence of the foreign graduate. In the last procedure, co-operation between the National Board of Medical Examiners and state licensing boards would be helpful. The problem is one calling for prompt and thoughtful action on the part of the medical profession and state licensing boards. A beginning has been made by the creation of a Joint Commission for the Evaluation of Foreign Medical Graduates in April, 1954, by representatives of nineteen national agencies, including federal bodies as well as state licensing boards.

The newly created Macy Foundation in 1930 began at once to assist agencies working for the improvement of medical education. In its first year it contributed toward a survey of methods and procedures in medical education in the United States and other countries conducted by the Commission on Medical Education of the Association of American Medical Colleges under the direction of Dr. Willard C. Rappleye.*
Medical schools in the early 1930's were facing many of the

* *Final Report of the Commission on Medical Education,* New York, 1932.

45

same problems that persist today: high costs of maintaining teaching and research facilities adequate for a university department; overcrowding of the curriculum because of the vast increase of medical knowledge; problems of relating teaching to research and undergraduate to graduate education; relating medical education on both levels to health care as a whole.

The Advisory Board for Medical Specialties, composed of representatives from each of the specialty boards approved by the Council on Medical Education and Hospitals of the American Medical Association, was organized in 1933-34. The Foundation contributed support to its studies directed toward standardization of requirements for medical specialties for several years.

A sequel to the report of the Commission on Medical Education was a study of graduate medical education made by the Commission on Graduate Medical Education organized by the Advisory Board for Medical Specialties in 1938 under the chairmanship of Dr. Willard C. Rappleye,* with assistance from the Foundation.

The Advisory Council on Medical Education, made up of representatives of some dozen organizations of medical colleges, hospitals, medical boards, medical specialties, and other scientific societies, was established in 1939 to co-ordinate the activities of those agencies in raising still higher the standards of medical education. The Foundation made grants to the Council in 1939, 1940, and 1944.

In 1941, 1942, and 1944, the Association of American Medical Colleges received grants from the Foundation for conferences and consultations dealing with problems growing out of the nation's war-time needs.

In direct relations with universities in the 1930's the Foundation gave substantial support to development of graduate medical education at the College of Physicians and Surgeons,

---

[1] *Graduate Medical Education,* University of Chicago Press, Chicago, 1940.

Columbia University, and made grants to Johns Hopkins University School of Medicine for a co-operative project between the Departments of Psychiatry and Pediatrics in a study of children in the Harriet Lane Home for Invalid Children and for another collaborative study between the Departments of Pharmacology and Internal Medicine; to Harvard Medical School for integration of teaching between the Departments of Physiology and Internal Medicine; to Syracuse University College of Medicine for a study of the application of the family case method to undergraduate medical education which showed students the importance of relating knowledge of the patient's social and economic environment to his medical problems for both diagnosis and treatment, and for a study by Dr. H. G. Weiskotten of graduates of the College at various periods after their entrance into practice.

When the war of 1941-45 made knowledge of tropical diseases an urgent necessity, the Foundation made a five-year grant to the College of Physicians and Surgeons, Columbia University, to establish a department of tropical medicine within the School of Public Health.

The Foundation's policy of assisting organizations devoted to improvement of medical education was directed to a new channel with the establishment of the National Fund for Medical Education in 1949. The Fund, created by the united efforts of leaders in industry, the medical profession, and public life, annually raises and distributes money to the approved medical schools of the country. It undertakes to interpret the needs of the medical schools to the public, to make it possible for the schools to maintain and advance their standards of education, to preserve academic freedom, and to offer equal opportunities to all qualified for the profession of medicine. The Fund has an advisory council of university presidents and the close co-operation of the Association of American Medical Colleges and the American Medical Association through its American Medical Education Foundation. It has appealed

47

to the nation's big industries, for their stake in medical progress is important. The medical profession has loyally supported the undertaking.

The Macy Foundation made a grant of $10,000 early in 1950 to help launch the Fund's program. The next year the Foundation joined eleven other agencies in providing for the administrative expenses of the Fund so that all the contributions it received from other sources could be devoted to the support of the teaching budgets of the medical schools. The Foundation continued its assistance with additional grants in 1952, 1953, and 1954.

The National Fund has met with gratifying success. In July, 1954, sums totaling $2,176,904, collected by the Fund and the American Medical Education Foundation, were distributed to the seventy-four approved medical schools and the six basic medical science schools of the country. These two organizations since 1951 have given nearly seven million dollars to the medical schools.* The partnership between medicine and industry is growing in strength, to the advantage of the nation's health. Congress gave recognition to the National Fund for Medical Education by granting it a federal charter in August, 1954.

A program of exchange of residents between the Columbia-Presbyterian Hospital Medical Center in New York and Guy's Hospital in London began in 1949, with the assistance of the Macy Foundation. Two physicians representing neurology and otolaryngology from each institution spent six months in the foreign hospital. The last month of the period was devoted to travel and study in other institutions in the country visited. The English residents included several medical centers in the United States and Canada in their visits and the Americans were able to travel on the Continent. The exchange residents

---

* "Medical Education in the United States and Canada, 54th Annual Report . . . by the Council on Medical Education and Hospitals of the American Medical Association," *Jour. Am. Med. Assoc.*, 1954, *156*, (Sept. 11), 137-176.

were drawn subsequently from the fields of internal medicine, surgery, pediatrics, obstetrics, and others.

After the first year of the program's operation, the Foundation made an additional and larger appropriation in 1950 to continue it. Through 1952 and part of 1953 the exchange proceeded; because of technicalities involved in practice regulations it was reluctantly abandoned.

The men who took part in the program on both sides of the Atlantic found the opportunity immeasurably valuable. Among the benefits they recorded were the widening of clinical experience, observation of new methods, seeing old problems from new points of view, getting to know men in their specialties whom they had previously known only through publications, working in institutions of another country for long enough time to see beneath the surface and learn how they actually function. To all the exchange residents the biggest gain was the insight they acquired into the ways of life of the other country, insight achieved by virtue of the warm friendships made with and through their colleagues in the host hospital.

The number of medical students who drop out of their training because of emotional disturbances has been a serious concern of medical schools in the United States for many years. Greater awareness of the problem has resulted in more careful attention to students' relation to the school, causes of failure, and reasons for leaving school.

The School of Medicine of the University of Texas appointed a committee, early in 1954, to consider students' difficulties and to suggest ways of helping them to make the adjustments required by the process of preparation for medical careers. The committee recommended a general study that would include correlation of the psychological profiles of students, derived by modern techniques, with records of academic performance and personal relations during the medical school period and even later, when the graduate had become a practicing physician. The program ideally should continue through ten to twenty years. Compiling of the profiles would start with group testing of all entering students by standard projective methods before class work had begun, to be followed by individual testing at greater length by a clinical psychologist. The data compiled through the course of the study would provide a basis for effective help in the student's adjustment and would be of value to the school's admissions officers in selection of candidates. Correlation of the results of the Texas study with similar studies being conducted by other medical schools would be of value to all concerned.

The new program of testing and guidance at the Texas School of Medicine has been set up as an adjunct to the student health service, with a part-time consulting psychiatrist added to the staff and a consulting psychologist to conduct the psychological studies and the counselling service as needed by students, their families, and the faculty.

The Macy Foundation made a five-year grant to the University of Texas, Medical Branch, beginning September 1, 1954, to support the program under the direction of Dr. Chauncey D. Leake, Executive Director of the Medical Branch.

Reports from the school after the academic year 1954-55 had begun announced that the psychological testing program was proceeding smoothly and had demonstrated a new correlation of the results of psychological tests with academic success or failure.

The New York Academy of Medicine in 1928 held the first Graduate Fortnight, a series of lectures by eminent specialists designed to bring to practicing physicians the latest developments in a selected area of medical knowledge. The Macy Foundation has had a somewhat proprietary interest in the Fortnight because the first one was instigated by Dr. Ludwig Kast, who later became the Foundation's first president. Since 1931, the Foundation has given assistance to the program on many occasions. In 1944 the Academy established the

Ludwig Kast Lectureship to open the series of lectures, demonstrations, and exhibitions each year. The Foundation has made support of the lectureship its annual contribution to the event.

The teaching of clinical medicine has undergone radical changes in the past fifty years. When Sir William Osler, at the new Johns Hopkins School of Medicine in the 1890's, took his students from the lecture room to the hospital bedside he carried the practical philosophy of the laboratory into the teaching of care of the sick. The next logical step came in the second decade of the twentieth century with the suggestion that professors of clinical subjects should be full-time members of the faculty as were the teachers of the laboratory subjects. The conflict aroused by this revolutionary step has not yet been resolved. Practical difficulties are formidable. Habits of mind firmly rooted in physicians through the long period of proprietary medical schools are not easily altered. Though the plan has been tried by many schools, it has not proved as feasible as its original proponents had hoped it would.

A complication of the problem now arises from the effect of prepayment for medical and hospital care and other forms of insurance upon the teaching of the clinical subjects in hospital and medical school. The new plans of arranging for payment through insurance programs bring problems to the administration of the teaching hospital which threaten to disturb the hospital-medical school relationship in many ways, both at the level of the resident training program and at the undergraduate level. The nation's health needs require the constant flow of well-trained physicians from our best teaching institutions. Medical insurance programs are a generally accepted social necessity. The co-ordination of the two needs must not be neglected.

The Council of Teaching Hospitals, composed of representatives of eight eastern university medical schools and their

51

affiliated hospitals, considered the problem at a meeting in New York in November, 1954. As a result of these discussions, the Macy Foundation agreed to support an informal conference to deal with the effect of prepayment and other forms of insurance plans on the programs of teaching hospitals and clinical departments of medical schools.

The Foundation's chief venture into post-graduate medical education is, of course, its conference program (see pages 13-25). In these informal gatherings investigators, practitioners, educators, and administrators make direct, intimate contact with others of different disciplines and with different professional experience, approach specific problems of common interest, share data and methods relating to work in progress, and greatly enrich their professional lives.

Many of the research projects aided by the Foundation include assistance to the training of investigators or clinicians in their execution. In Europe, the laboratories of Dr. Nine Choucroun in France, Dr. Paul Govaerts and Dr. Corneille Heymans in Belgium, and Dr. Tage Astrup in Denmark are centers in which young investigators are working under the direction of leaders in scientific research. In New York, Dr. Elaine P. Ralli, whose work on adrenal cortex the Foundation has assisted for some years, has had a number of young physicians working as assistants in her research. She has also enabled carefully chosen members of the New York University College of Medicine fourth-year medical classes to work on her research project as an elective activity. The Columbia University research division at Goldwater Memorial Hospital offers clinical training in chronic disabilities to fourth-year students from other medical schools as well as from the classes of the College of Physicians and Surgeons. Dr. Donald H. Barron's program of research on the physiology of pregnancy in animals being conducted at Yale University School of Medicine includes provision for training. Dr. Barron has found the participation of young investigators working with him to be of great assistance to his project, and he believes that a year's training in such a program as his and Dr. C. Sidney Burwell's at Harvard would be useful to students who plan to enter the fields of medicine, pediatrics, and obstetrics.

# THE HEALTH OF THE COMMUNITY

WHEN the Macy Foundation began its activities, economic dislocations that were to last for several years were turning the minds of the public as well as of the medical and social work professions urgently to the high costs of adequate medical care. Not only the low-income groups, but many who had been able to pay for what they needed before were finding the costs of medical service hard to meet; hospitals and medical schools faced curtailed income; doctors were underpaid. New services to supplement clinical medicine had grown up in the years before 1930: family casework expanded and improved by medical and psychiatric social work, public health programs, child guidance, school health counseling, industrial health services, vocational and educational guidance, parent education and family consultation, and others. Many of these functions were so new that they were still struggling to overcome public apathy if not resistance. With financial troubles plaguing every public and private agency for human welfare, ways of improving these services, integrating them, and placing them at the disposal of the greatest number offered an opportunity for the ventures of a new philanthropy.

In 1930 and 1931, the Foundation gave funds to the Committee on Costs of Medical Care; the next year it contributed to a survey of facilities for the care of the chronically ill made by the Welfare Council of New York City.* Later it made several grants to a study of all hospitals in the New York metropolitan area conducted by the United Hospital Fund of New York.† Following the revelation of inadequacies of

---

* Jarrett, Mary C., *Chronic Illness in New York City*, Columbia University Press, New York, 1933, 2 volumes.
† Survey Staff and Collaborating Individuals and Associations, *Report of the Hospital Survey for New York*, New York, 1937, 3 volumes.

the provisions for care of convalescent patients made by this study, the New York Academy of Medicine held two conferences on convalescent care in 1939 and 1944. The Foundation supported both.*

In 1940-1942, the Foundation assisted a study of health needs in a group of New York City families made by Earl L. Koos of the Department of Sociology of Columbia University,† and contributed to a collaborative project by the Cornell University Medical College, New York Hospital, and Community Service Society studying the family in relation to sickness and health care in the Kips Bay Yorkville Health District. A grant to the Research Council of the New York City Department of Hospitals in 1945 provided for publication of a volume describing the development of the chronic disease program at Welfare Island.‡

Development of group practice units at Montefiore Hospital and at the New York University College of Medicine as part of the Health Insurance Plan of Greater New York received assistance from the Foundation between 1945 and 1952.

In 1943, the Foundation made a grant to Neighborhood Health Development, Inc., of New York for a study of medical care for the moderate income groups of New York, carried out by the Mayor's Committee.

Joining other foundations, the Macy Foundation supported a study group at the New York Academy of Medicine, the Committee on Medicine and the Changing Order, which met weekly for three years to consider all phases of medical science and practice. The committee summarized its findings in a series of monographs in the late 1940's, each one devoted to

---

* *Convalescent Care, Proceedings of the Conference . . . November 9 and 10, 1939*, New York Academy of Medicine, New York, 1940; *Convalescence and Rehabilitation, Proceedings of the Conference . . April 25-26, 1944*, New York Academy of Medicine, New York, 1944.

† Koos, Earl Lomon, *Families in Trouble*, King's Crown Press, New York, 1946.

‡ *Research, An Experiment in Municipal Organization. Goldwater Memorial Hospital*, Department of Hospitals, City of New York, 1945

a particular aspect of the changes taking place in the theory and practice of medicine.

As part of its centennial celebration in the spring of 1947, the New York Academy of Medicine held three-day institutes on social, medical, and public health; the Foundation contributed to their support.

## Administrative Medicine

Events of the years in which a long and severe economic depression was followed by the most devastating war in history brought to the people of this nation a realization of the necessity of health services for the individual and the community. Public commissions and privately supported groups studied the existing conditions of these services and the directions in which they could be expanded and improved. Lawmakers provided more funds for research and care. New problems of health care created by the rapid advances of medical science and by the socio-economic developments that have made those advances possible call for joint efforts of medical and social agencies for their solution.

Forms and methods of medical care are rapidly evolving in unpredictable directions. The only clear fact is that there will continue to be change. Inquiry, experimentation, and training must be devoted to development of administration of facilities, personnel, and program with the aim of eventually making available to the entire populace the knowledge and skill developing so rapidly in laboratory and clinic.

Certain trends in contemporary American life foreshadow some of the modifications likely to come about in health and medical care. One has to do with the role of the physician. He is today, as he has been since the days of Hippocrates, the individual's first defense in the protection of his health. But the doctor has now become the central figure in a team of nurses, dieticians, dentists, social workers, psychologists, physical therapists, pharmacists, technicians of many kinds,

57

and a number of specialists.* It is his responsibility to guide the patient through the labyrinthine health organization.

The trend toward specialization has been inexorable during the years in which medical knowledge has grown to such immensity that no one person could possibly master it. There are about three times as many specialties recognized today as there were in the 1920's, and the proportion of medical school graduates who enter the specialties instead of general practice has increased markedly in recent decades. Internists tend to specialize within their field, as they center their interests upon cardiology, hematology, gastroenterology, or some other study area. There is a widely held belief that the general practitioner should actually be a specialist, trained for the role of family physician – a combination of internist and psychiatrist or psychologist. The development of specialization is unquestionably desirable, for it has greatly advanced knowledge and improved the quality of medical care available, but it must be accompanied by development of teamwork, whether through the device of group practice or other means.

The activities of the health team are based in the hospital, no longer merely a place where patients too ill to be about or to be cared for in their homes are provided for, but a center of diagnostic, preventive, and therapeutic services, community health services, research, and medical education. The demands upon the nation's hospitals have increased so greatly in recent years that; although their capacity has grown, they cannot meet the needs.

The kinds of care the hospital is called upon to give have changed radically. Modern preventive and therapeutic techniques have reduced or entirely eliminated need for hospitalization of patients for many infectious diseases that once filled hospital beds. But as the proportion of old people increases, there is ever greater need for hospitals to provide longer-term

---

* There are more than forty functionally different services ministering to the preventive and curative needs of the citizen. Most of them have formed their own associations and set up their own standards of practice.

care for persons suffering from the chronic and degenerative diseases that incapacitate the elderly and make them a burden upon their families. Hospitals, already crowded with these patients, must create and expand facilities for care, treatment, and rehabilitation of the chronically ill. Experience has shown that convalescence and rehabilitation of the elderly patient, even more than of the younger patient, are hastened by treatment that gets him out of the hospital bed and back in his home as quickly as possible. Improved techniques for accomplishing this will relieve the burden on the hospital and help prevent much wasteful invalidism.

Prevention of illness is approached in several ways. There is the preventive medicine practiced by the public health agencies that has done so much to wipe out epidemics in the past fifty years. There is the prevention of serious illness or complication accomplished by the watchful physician through early detection and accurate diagnosis. And there is the hospital's success in preventing recurrence of illness or development of sequelae of many diseases.* Development of the hospital's preventive functions has required expansion of diagnostic and other laboratories, out-patient services, and clinics as more patients formerly hospitalized are now treated satisfactorily on an ambulatory basis. The out-patient sections also are the ones through which the hospital's health services, including public education, most logically develop and are

---

* The Syracuse University College of Medicine program of family case method for fourth-year students during their service on the hospital wards (see p. 47), supported by the Foundation in the 1930's, led to another study, also with help from the Foundation, of what could be accomplished by providing medical and social-work care of the chronically ill ward patients after discharge from the hospital. A program of follow-up care by an extramural resident and a social worker was begun while the patient was still in the hospital. The extramural resident acted as the family physician of the discharged patient. The program resulted in a notable reduction of rehospitalization and a consequent lightening of the financial burden on the community. (See Jensen, F., Weiskotten, H. G., and Thomas, Margaret A., *Medical Care of the Discharged Hospital Patient,* Commonwealth Fund, New York, 1944.)

carried out in co-operation with community health departments and voluntary agencies.

The rapid growth of plans for prepayment of medical services has had pronounced effect on hospital programs. These plans ease the financial load of the hospital, but they have also taxed hospital capacity and personnel by making possible hospital care for many who could not otherwise afford it. They create problems of hospital organization and function that call for solutions by skilled medical administrators.

The hospital has always been an indispensable part of medical education. In addition to its functions in the formal training of physicians, surgeons, nurses, and technicians, the hospital has a still wider educational mission. The practitioner of medicine or surgery, whose education continues throughout his professional life, finds the hospital wards, clinics, laboratories, and association with his colleagues on the staff his main reliance in keeping abreast of medical progress.

The research function of the hospital is the one with which the public is least familiar. It usually comes to general attention only with the announcement of a discovery or some other newsworthy feat. The research sections are now, however, a major feature of all teaching hospitals. The laboratories of the teaching hospital of a university medical school have the advantage of close affiliation with the laboratories of the medical school and of other schools of the university. In these great centers of learning, the accretion of medical knowledge goes on with progressive acceleration.

Co-ordination of all the elements of modern health care facilities calls for a new member of the medical team: the medical administrator. There have been administrators of hospitals and public health programs since those institutions came into existence, but they have been concerned with administration only of the institution with which they were affiliated. The new administrator must be capable of integration on a larger scale. He must be a specialist in imaginative planning of programs and in bringing together and guiding the personnel to execute the programs. Just what his training and personal qualifications should be are matters still being studied by leaders in many of the professions concerned.

The Foundation welcomed the opportunity to assist a program of research and teaching in the field of medical and health care administration when Columbia University established its Institute of Administrative Medicine. Organized under the University's School of Public Health, the Institute began its operation on January 1, 1952. With the University's departments of law, business, economics, sociology, engineering, and others available for co-operation in areas where their skills touch the health care field, and with New York's many hospitals, public health facilities, and voluntary agencies to serve as resources for study of community health problems, the Institute undertook exploration, teaching, and research.

In the next three years, the new department organized a faculty, developed a course in hospital administration that is now well established, and worked out curricula for students interested in medical prepayment, occupational medicine, and Blue Cross administration.

The faculty of the Institute and of the School of Public Health directed and participated in a number of studies of organization and effectiveness of hospital and other health services in the vicinity of New York City and in other localities. The findings of these studies have been used as teaching material in the Institute's courses; when published, they will serve even more widely as source material for study and teaching of administrative medicine.

Early in 1955, the University Trustees, recognizing the importance of administrative medicine and the accomplishments of the Institute, announced that the School of Public Health would henceforth be named the School of Public Health and Administrative Medicine.

## Conference on Administrative Medicine

Other universities and medical centers have initiated programs of research, teaching, and organization in administrative medicine. To bring together leaders in the movement, the Foundation organized a conference group on Administrative Medicine which held its first meeting in March, 1953, another in December of the same year, and a third in October, 1954. Members of the group were chosen from public health teaching and administration; hospital administration; health insurance and group practice; nursing; medical education and practice; labor organization; psychiatry; and sociology. Three had served on the President's Commission on Health Needs of the Nation in 1951. Guests brought other interests to the discussions.

The conferences have studied the field of medical and health care administration, the functions of the administrator and his necessary qualifications, training for the various types of administrator, the roles of medical and non-medical persons in medical administration, and other phases of the general problem. The first three meetings of the group have made an encouraging beginning in exploring a field that is not so much new as it is vastly more complex than ever before, and toward pointing out the specific needs for research, teaching, and integration within it.

# THE WHOLE PATIENT

MEDICINE as a science and an art has now come full circle, from concern with man as the basic unit to interest in organs and systems of the body, then to study of the cell, and now at last back to recognition of man as an indivisible unit of mind and body. The medicine man or priest of not so many centuries ago treated the sick person, not the specific organs or functions involved in the ailment. Toward the end of the eighteenth century the belief that certain organs were the seat of diseases came into acceptance. At the beginning of the era of scientific medicine as we know it – the publication of Virchow's theory of cellular pathology in 1858 – the cell, which had already been recognized as the unit of plant life, became the center of medical attention. When Pasteur and Koch demonstrated the existence of pathogenic bacteria, medical scientists concentrated their attention upon the effects of the invasion of the body by these organisms, the pathological changes occurring in tissues and resultant disturbances of function. Other external causes of change in structure and function were recognized, and animal experimentation became the method by which the nature of the changes could be studied and remedies developed.

This was the stage at which medicine attained the status of a science, with its practitioners and investigators jealously guarding what they conceived to be the true nature of its right to that status: strict objectivity of judgment and testing of hypotheses by laboratory methods.

The concern with scientific methods led to further specialization and reliance by the specialists on quantitative measurements and other laboratory tests. Thus medical care was more and more divided between the family physician and the specialist, the former too busy and the latter too preoccupied

63

with his "science" to listen to the patient's recital of fears and worries, often the most important clues to the nature of his illness. The impersonal attitude was the rule in medical school and hospital, and the patient's history and treatment were scattered among a number of doctors and clinics. When a group of five hundred physicians five to twelve years out of medical school was queried, in about 1930, about the relative value of their medical studies, many recorded their dissatisfaction with their preparation to deal with patients from a human viewpoint, to correlate and interpret all the data about the various facets of the patient's life.*

Proof of the influence of emotions upon body functions came into medical lore from a respected branch of medical science: physiology. The research of Pavlov on conditioned reflexes, the investigations and teachings of Dr. Walter B. Cannon of Harvard and of his pupils demonstrated as scientifically as could be wished that physiological processes, specifically visceral functions, and emotions could be correlated experimentally. Dr. Cannon studied the mechanisms by which the body avoids or corrects internal disequilibriums. His findings were applied to human biology, and mechanisms similar to those observed in experimental animals were traced in human beings. From physiology, too, came a vast amount of knowledge of the functions of the endocrine glands, their relation to the behavior of other organs and systems, and the interdependence of endocrine glands and emotions.

At the time of the Macy Foundation's establishment there had been a decade or more of increasing awareness that emotions were an important factor in the production of disease and a growing willingness on the part of physicians to take account of that factor. The term "psychosomatic medicine," admittedly imperfect but useful, was coming into use to designate the study of the interrelations between the psychological and physiological aspects of normal and abnormal bodily

---

* *Final Report of the Commission on Medical Education,* New York, 1932, 255.

functions. The psychosomatic approach was a modern application of a long-known truth — that a person is composed indivisibly of mind and body — and an enlargement of the knowledge of the whole person. Investigators had shown that factors of which the patient is unconscious influence physiological processes quite as surely and unmistakably as they do total outward behavior. With this concept gaining acceptance in the minds of practitioners, medical care was profoundly affected. Once again the care of the patient was being centered in the hands of one man; the doctor was to resume his original function of treating the whole man, not his organs or his diseases as separate entities.

With their donor's broad definition of health and interest in the integration of biological and psychological knowledge to guide them, the Directors and officers of the Macy Foundation began at once to assist projects in the general area of psychosomatic problems. In 1931 they sponsored a survey of the world's literature on the relation of emotion to disease published in 1935 as *Emotion and Bodily Changes* by Dr. H. Flanders Dunbar (Columbia University Press, New York; later editions in 1938, 1946, and 1954). With this survey as a background, the Department of Practice of Medicine (now Department of Medicine) of the College of Physicians and Surgeons, Columbia University, collaborating with the Department of Psychiatry and Surgery, made a psychosomatic study of patients suffering from cardiovascular disturbances, rheumatic fever, diabetes, and repeated accidental injuries. The Foundation gave support to the study for several years beginning in 1934. The results were published in Dr. Dunbar's book, *Psychosomatic Diagnosis* (Paul B. Hoeber, Inc., New York, 1943).

Other projects in this area assisted by the Foundation in the 1930's were: a study of sympathetic responses in young children conducted by Teachers College, Columbia University; an investigation of the development of personality in childhood

65

at the Institute of Human Relations, Yale University; experimental studies of the neural basis of emotional expression, throwing light on the interrelationships between the central nervous system and the vegetative nervous system, under Dr. Philip Bard first at Harvard Medical School and later at the Johns Hopkins University School of Medicine; an investigation of social, economic, and environmental factors in disease conducted by Dr. G. Canby Robinson in the Department of Medicine of the Johns Hopkins University School of Medicine; a study by Dr. Bela Mittelmann and Dr. Harold G. Wolff at the Cornell University Medical College, Department of Medicine, concerning the influence of emotion upon the peripheral circulation; investigations of disturbances of consciousness and of convulsive disorders by means of biochemical and bioelectrical techniques by Dr. F. A. Gibbs and Dr. W. G. Lennox in the Departments of Physiology and Neurology, Harvard Medical School; a psychosomatic study of surgical shock under the direction of Dr. E. D. Churchill and Dr. Stanley Cobb representing a collaboration between the Departments of Surgery and Neuropathology of the Harvard Medical School at the Massachusetts General Hospital; studies of the relation of the pattern of electrical brain waves to the structure of personality under the direction of Dr. Hallowell Davis at Harvard Medical School, Department of Physiology.

Other studies of psychosomatic problems supported by the Foundation in the late 1930's were one by Dr. Carl Binger with the collaboration of Dr. Alfred E. Cohn at the Hospital of the Rockefeller Institute for Medical Research under the auspices of the New York Tuberculosis and Health Association and the New York Heart Association on the personality of patients suffering from vascular hypertension; an investigation of the physiological functioning of preadolescents to reveal early stages of psychosomatic dysfunctioning, under the direction of Dr. Nathan W. Shock at the University of California's Institute of Child Welfare; and development of more efficient methods of history taking to reveal the patient's conflicts and anxieties without his awareness of the process by Dr. Felix Deutsch at the Harvard Medical School and later at the Washington University School of Medicine. Dr. Deutsch's method, which he called "associative anamnesis" and used especially in studies of allergic and skin reactions, is applicable also to investigations of many organic disturbances and has been helpful in teaching medical students and social workers to use the psychosomatic approach.

To promote knowledge of human psychosomatic problems by means of animal experimentation, the Foundation began in 1937 to support Dr. Howard S. Liddell's studies of experimental neuroses in animals conducted at Cornell University. An investigator dividing his time between Dr. Liddell's laboratory and the Harvard Medical School created a link between the animal studies and those of Dr. Stanley Cobb on human patients.

The journal *Psychosomatic Medicine* was established in 1939 to provide a medium for the publication of studies in the field. Its editorial board represented internal medicine, pediatrics, experimental psychology, psychiatry, physiology, and other disciplines. The Foundation, through a grant to the National Research Council, helped the undertaking, which continues to be an important channel of communication. It has been adopted as the official organ of the American Society for Research in Psychosomatic Medicine, formed in 1942.

Between 1940 and 1950, the Foundation made grants totalling $207,000 to sixteen universities and research institutions to support research and education in psychosomatic medicine. Among the projects were the studies of Dr. Harold G. Wolff and Dr. Stewart Wolf of the Cornell University Medical College on a patient with an opening through the abdominal wall into the stomach similar to the historic work of Dr. William Beaumont on Alexis St. Martin of a century ago, the modern study revealing the influence of emotional factors on the functioning of the stomach, particularly in the formation of peptic ulcers; Dr. Hilde Bruch's studies of obesity in childhood conducted at the College of Physicians and Surgeons, Columbia University, demonstrating that the attitudes of obese children and their families toward food habits and other factors in the home environment have more to do with children's excessive eating than does the imbalance of the endocrine glands; the studies of the use of hypnosis in the investigation and treatment of neuropsychiatric and psychosomatic disturbances carried on at the Menninger Foundation by Dr. Margaret Brenman and Dr. Merton M. Gill for three years and resulting in the publication of their book, *Hypnotherapy, A Survey of the Literature* (International Universities Press, New York, 1947), an investigation later enlarged under grants from the United States Public Health Service; a three-year study of hypnosis as a procedure for the relief of psychosomatic disorders carried on at the College of Physicians and Surgeons, Columbia University, Department of Neurology, under the direction of Dr. Lawrence S. Kubie, in which he developed a method of using the rhythmic sounds of the patient's breathing, amplified, to induce hypnotic sleep and recall of forgotten traumatic occurrences.

The Foundation supported (1939-1941) a comprehensive project by Cornell University Medical College, the New York Hospital, and the Community Service Society to study the family as a health-care unit, a group seen from the point of view of the hospital, the physician, the social worker, and the anthropologist. The material accumulated by the investigators demonstrated the effects of family tensions upon individual members — psychosomatic disturbances in some, and in others emotional maladjustments leading to failure, delinquency, or crime. The publication resulting from the study was *Patients Have Families*, by Henry B. Richardson (The Commonwealth Fund, New York, 1945). Another investigation of the occurrence of psychosomatic disturbances in delinquents and criminals and in their families conducted by Dr. David Abrahamsen, of the Department of Psychiatry, College of

Physicians and Surgeons, Columbia University, with Foundation support from 1945 through 1948, and with co-operation from the New York State Department of Probation, brought forth information of such value that Dr. Abrahamsen was later asked to direct a twenty-month study of the causes of sex crime at Sing Sing prison. Following the completion of the study, a program of individual and group therapy for the rehabilitation of sex criminals was begun at the prison and a bill, based on Dr. Abrahamsen's recommendations, was passed by the New York legislature giving judges the power to sentence sex offenders to indeterminate terms so that those who respond to treatment may be released when rehabilitation is judged successful and those who do not may be imprisoned for life, if necessary to protect the public.

For three years, 1947 through 1949, the Foundation supported the publication in two widely read journals, *The Practitioner* and *The American Journal of Medicine*, of a series of case histories of patients in the psychiatric and pediatric wards of the Massachusetts General Hospital under the direction of Dr. Stanley Cobb and Dr. Allan M. Butler. The histories provided invaluable teaching material for undergraduate and graduate medical students and made available to practicing physicians information about the modern methods of diagnosis and treatment of psychosomatic disturbances. Published in book form in 1952,* the case histories and accompanying discussions by attending staff members show how much can be accomplished by close teamwork among the surgeon, internist, psychiatrist, psychologist, and social worker in dealing with the great variety of psychosomatic problems encountered in a general hospital.

The physician has always served as a family counsellor in times of trouble. The services of doctor and minister at such times touch and supplement each other in many respects. A

---

* *Case Histories in Psychosomatic Medicine*, edited by Henry H W. Miles, M D , Stanley Cobb, M.D., and Harley C Shands, M.D., W. W Norton and Company, New York, 1952.

movement to bring them into closer rapport has been going on in the United States and Great Britain for many years.

The New York Academy of Medicine's Committee on Ministry and Medicine has long been concerned with effecting understanding and communication between the two professions. Resuming an early interest in the subject, the Foundation contributed to the holding of two conferences on Ministry and Medicine in Human Relationships held by the Academy committee on May 11, 1950, and April 18-19, 1952. On both occasions a group of teachers of theology, pastors, specialists in pastoral care, clinically trained chaplains met with psychiatrists, internists, and general practitioners. They discussed the normal experiences of human life in which the ministry is concerned and the disabilities and maladjustments for which the pastor should have medical or psychiatric assistance in working with his charges. The purpose of the conference was to emphasize the overlapping of functions of the two professions and to show how each can assist the other in carrying out its duties. Sympathetic and understanding cooperation between the curator of man's spiritual nature and the physician who protects his mental and bodily health completes the provision for care of the whole human creature.

# THE LIFE CYCLE

PARALLEL to the concept of man as a psychosomatic unit, and inseparable from it, there is the time-honored and still meaningful emphasis upon the life history of the individual and the species as an approach to understanding man's nature and needs. All the life sciences make their contributions to full study of the stages through which the individual develops from a microscopic organism to maturity as a human being, suffers the deteriorations of age, and comes to the end of his life. Investigations of the processes of biological growth (understood not just as change in size, but also as differentiation and organization of inherent potentialities) must include systematic study of the effect of experience upon the development of the organism as it takes on individuality. Through observation and experiment, scientists can acquire knowledge of the integration of structure and function that produces the individual's susceptibilities and resistances to disease, idiosyncrasies of behavior, and the unique combinations of characteristics that give him his creative potentialities.

The Macy Foundation has always been interested in this longitudinal synthesis, and has therefore supported studies in genetics, the processes of heredity, ovulation, embryology, growth at different stages of life, child development, maturation, and problems of aging.

## Early Development

Among the Foundation's earliest grants were several to the Neurological Institute of the Columbia-Presbyterian Medical Center for research into the development of behavior in man conducted in its Normal Child Development Clinic, established in 1931. Behavior was defined, for the purposes of these investigations, as the neuromuscular and glandular reactions

71

of living human organisms, and basic studies of behavior in fetal and postnatal life were made to learn as much as possible of the growth and development of the central nervous system.

The Foundation suggested to Dr. Frederick Tilney, who was directing the research, that a survey of current literature on fetal and infant development would be of great value to the program and offered to finance such a survey. The result was the volume *Behavior Development in Infants* by Evelyn Dewey published by the Columbia University Press in 1935. Studies of the developmental sequences of infant behavior were published the same year in Myrtle B. McGraw's *Growth: A Study of Johnny and Jimmy* (D. Appleton-Century, New York).

The zoologist-anatomist Dr. George E. Coghill, devoting himself to research and teaching from the early years of the century to a period shortly before his death in 1941, made observations on the growth of the nervous system and its relation to the earliest development of embryonic behavior that have become classics of biological lore and the point of departure for most studies of animal and human behavior made since his work won wide recognition. One of his most fundamental observations was that behavior first appears as a total reaction of the organism, and that the smaller patterns, or specific reflexes, come about through a process of individuation from the total pattern. The Macy Foundation takes pride in having assisted Dr. Coghill's research, first at the Wistar Institute of Anatomy and Biology in Philadelphia, and later in his private laboratory in Florida.*

Studies in mammalian genetics made under the direction of Dr. C. C. Little at the Roscoe B. Jackson Memorial Laboratory at Bar Harbor, Maine, in the 1930's received Foundation support and made valuable contributions to the knowledge of heredity, the growth process, and the interrelationship of the glands of internal secretion. The influence of hormonal activities on the behavior of lower vertebrates was studied by Dr.

---

<sup>1</sup> See pages 90-91 and 117.

G. Kingsley Noble at the American Museum of Natural History, with Foundation support in the 1930's.*

The physical development of the animal organism is most rapid and least understood in its earliest stages. Scientists are ignorant of the nature of the events immediately following fertilization of the human ovum, of the force that within some two hundred eighty days transforms the ovum into a healthy, crying infant, and of the same events and the same vital force at work in the twenty-one days of the chick's life within the egg.

Among research projects assisted by the Foundation in its early years were attempts to learn something of the natural laws governing the first steps of the transformation of a mass of apparently identical cells into a highly complex organism with all the traits of its kind. One of these was the research on factors affecting growth and differentiation of the mammalian embryo done at the Columbia University Department of Zoology under the direction of Dr. Leslie C. Dunn. Dr. Salome Gluecksohn, working with Dr. Dunn, developed a method of transplanting mouse embryos at very early stages into the membranes of growing chick embryos, a technique that made it possible to study the mammalian embryo outside the uterus under controlled experimental conditions. It was an important step in the development of experimental mammalian embryology.

Another project was the investigation of the physiology of mammalian eggs conducted by Dr. Gregory Pincus at Harvard University, with Foundation support from 1935 to 1938. Dr. Pincus and his assistants perfected techniques for the cultivation of rabbit and human eggs in vitro, for the transfer of eggs into suitable recipients, and for the study of cleavage and growth rates both in vivo and in vitro. They made observations on the process of fertilization and of parthenogenetic activation and compared the cytology and degrees of development attained by normal and artificial activation. Their studies

---

* See pages 90, 91.

73

of hormonal control of early development and factors originating with ovarian hormones produced a considerable set of informative data and techniques that were applied successfully to other problems in other institutions.

Continuing his studies at the Worcester Foundation for Experimental Biology, Dr. Pincus and his associates have shown that a biochemical factor normally supplied by the maternal fallopian tube is necessary for the fertilization of the rabbit egg. They hope to learn the chemical nature of the sperm-ripening agent. Dr. Pincus is also investigating the enzyme systems within living embryos that provide the energy for growth and differentiation. It appears that the early stages of growth are greatly influenced by the maternal hormones, especially those of the ovary. Dr. M. C. Chang, one of Dr. Pincus' colleagues, has developed technical methods, particularly the use of low temperatures to retard the growth of early embryos and to make possible the storage of ova, that will be of use in new studies of embryonic development.

The Macy Foundation resumed support of Dr. Pincus' investigations of the biochemistry and physiology of early growth and development of mammals by making a four-year grant to the Worcester Foundation for Experimental Biology in 1954. Among the results Dr. Pincus hopes to attain is a method of preventing certain congenital defects resulting from abnormalities in the physiology and biochemistry of the mother that are reflected adversely upon the embryo in its earliest and most vulnerable stages.

### Studies in Pregnancy

During the nine months of pregnancy, a number of major adaptations take place in the mother's body functions. Changes occur in circulation, in water balance and kidney function, in nutritional requirements, in hormonal balance (particularly striking because the placenta secretes a series of hormones to reinforce those normally produced), in blood chemistry, and in psychological attitude. These adaptive processes are not well understood even in normal pregnancy; when disease complicates them, they present still more acute problems. Systematic research on human pregnancy has been scant until recent years because the necessary technical methods had not been developed.

In 1950, the Harvard University Medical School set up a research laboratory at the Boston Lying-in Hospital under the direction of Dr. C. Sidney Burwell, Research Professor of Clinical Medicine. Dr. Burwell, who some years before had studied the cardiac burden imposed by pregnancy, has pursued his research and extended it to include the whole question of maternal adaptations. With a staff representing physiology, biochemistry, pathology, and internal medicine, and with close relations with the full-time members of the school's Department of Obstetrics, Dr. Burwell is conducting a long-range study of many problems involved in pregnancy. A five-year grant from the Foundation will help support the study from 1954 to 1959.

Dr. Burwell and his associates are continuing an investigation of the respiratory adjustments to pregnancy which they had started some time ago. They are also studying the physiological adjustments to labor. The volume of blood flow through the pregnant uterus is another subject of research. Knowledge of that point will make possible calculations of the oxygen consumption of the fetus in utero, heretofore difficult to establish. The group are making a systematic study of a number of pregnant women with heart disease, whose adaptation to the physiological demands of pregnancy are limited by cardiac weakness.

At the Yale University School of Medicine Dr. Donald H. Barron, Professor of Physiology, has been studying the physiology of pregnancy in mammals for some years. His investigations are concerned chiefly with the nature of the functional stress involved in the pregnant animal's providing for the needs of the fetus and the compensatory mechanisms involved in the process. Dr. Barron has worked out techniques for the study of the living fetus within the living maternal organism. He hopes to develop methods and apparatus for the maintenance of the fetus within the uterus completely separated from the mother animal, which would make possible more thorough study of the physiology and biochemistry of the uterus, placenta, and living fetus.

Dr. Burwell and his associates at Harvard have made repeated visits to Dr. Barron's laboratory during the past few years, comparing their studies of human pregnancy with the observations of the Yale group on pregnancy in rabbits, sheep, and goats. It is expected that the two groups will work in even closer co-operation in the future.

The Foundation made a five-year grant for support of Dr. Barron's research program in the fall of 1954.

Another study of pregnancy in which the emphasis is on the effects of disease is being conducted at the University of Louvain, Belgium. Dr. Joseph-Pierre Hoet, head of the Department of Internal Medicine, is investigating the effects of diabetes on the course of pregnancy and on the offspring. He has found a tendency toward endocrine imbalance, with excessive function of the adrenal cortex, and a serious abnormality of carbohydrate metabolism in pregnant women who suffer from or are predisposed to diabetes. These conditions produce a pathological environment for the developing embryo and often lead to miscarriage, resorption of the fetus, or congenital abnormalities in the child.

Professor Hoet has produced diabetes in rabbits and rats, which enabled him to study the carbohydrate disturbance of pregnant animals and the defects appearing in their offspring. He is developing methods of prevention of such defects in animals and man.

The Foundation is assisting Dr. Hoet's clinical and experimental studies with a four-year grant made in 1954.

## Gestation Conference

Many basic problems of biology and of human physical and mental health still inadequately understood lie in the general field of reproduction and early development. The Foundation hopes to explore the area with even greater thoroughness in the coming years as it executes its founder's mandate to seek out problems that "require for their solution studies and efforts in correlated fields . . . such as biology and the social sciences." The geneticist, the physiologist, the biochemist, the enzyme chemist, the anatomist, the experimental embryologist, the zoologist, the psychiatrist, the sociologist, the obstetrician, and the family physician can contribute to the solutions of these problems.

In the spring of 1954, a new Foundation conference group held its first meeting: the group on Gestation. Members represent the disciplines of physiology, anatomy, biology, biochemistry, zoology, obstetrics, gynecology, pathology, and psychiatry. Among them are Dr. Pincus, Dr. Barron, and Dr. Claude A. Villée, an associate of Dr. Burwell.

## Personality Development in Children

The Foundation has given assistance to programs related to the development of a healthy personality in children from its first years. In the 1930's, grants to Sarah Lawrence College, Vassar College, and Yale University supported studies of child personality.

The Foundation's conference group on Problems of Early Infancy held its first meeting in March, 1947, bringing a multi-discipline approach to problems of prenatal care, infancy, and the child's relationships within the family. Later changing its name to Problems of Infancy and Childhood, the group continued its productive meetings until 1953.*

Recognizing that study of the abnormal often provides clues to understanding of the normal, the Foundation made a grant in 1930 to the Department of Pediatrics of Johns Hopkins

------

See page 112

University School of Medicine for a full-time psychiatric consultation service at the Harriet Lane Home for Invalid Children to study psychopathological problems of childhood. This collaboration between pediatricians and psychiatrists, supported by the Foundation for three years, produced Dr. Leo Kanner's book *Child Psychiatry* (Charles C. Thomas, Baltimore, 1935).

## Emotional Development and Psychosexual Adjustment in Children with Endocrine Disorders

Children with endocrine disorders, especially those resulting in either precocious or retarded sexual development, present an unusual opportunity to evaluate the relative influence of intrinsic and environmental factors on the development of the individual's personality. In most cases of sexual abnormalities originating in endocrine derangement the patient can be restored to normal condition with dramatic rapidity either by operation to remove the overactive gland or by hormonal therapy to supply the endocrine deficiency.

The Endocrine Clinic for Children of the Johns Hopkins Hospital possesses a wealth of material for an investigation of a number of problems related to the role of hormones in emotional development, especially in the psychosexual area. In 1951 the Foundation made a three-year grant to the Johns Hopkins University School of Medicine to support a study of the emotional development and psychosexual adjustment of children suffering from endocrine disorders, with special reference to response to therapy. Under the direction of Dr. John C. Whitehorn, Professor of Psychiatry, a team of psychologists and psychiatrists has been studying various aspects of the physiological, psychological, and social readjustments made by such children as their bodies and feelings become normal under treatment. Dr. Lawson Wilkins, Chief of the Endocrine Clinic, has been directing correlated studies of the patients.

At the completion of the three-year period results showed that the study had been rewarding beyond anticipation. The number of children with endocrine disorders coming to the Johns Hopkins clinic from many parts of the country and the variety of their problems gave ample basis for observation. The clinic's successful treatments had aroused great interest among physicians. Patients studied fell generally into the following categories: 1) hermaphroditism; 2) sexual precocity; 3) eunochoidism; 4) failure of ovarian development. Cases of other kinds of sexual maldevelopment caused by disturbances of the thyroid, pituitary, adrenal, and parathyroid glands appeared from time to time.

Convinced of the value of the investigation and of the promise it held out for help in understanding psychopathic sexual behavior in adults as well as of children's problems, the Foundation renewed the grant for another three years in 1954.

An interesting development of the study was a bit of cooperation between the Johns Hopkins University group and the University of Pennsylvania's Department of Pediatrics. Dr. Paul György, through discussion with the Foundation's medical director of a remarkable case of congenital sexual malformation under treatment at the University of Pennsylvania Hospital, arranged to send the child to the Johns Hopkins Hospital for observation by Dr. Whitehorn's group. Following her stay there, Dr. György and Dr. Whitehorn and their associates held an inter-university seminar in Philadelphia in January, 1954, at which the subject of diagnosis and treatment of genetic intersexuality was discussed by members of both groups.

## Aging

One of the conspicuous facts in our nation today is the great and growing proportion of persons over the age of sixty-five, a fact that has already had marked influence on our social and economic life and will have more as improved health care prolongs the life span. The problems of caring for older people who are ill in mind or body and of providing suitable occupations for those who are still able to work, though pushed out of employment promptly at an arbitrary retirement age, are already pressing upon government, industry, and community leaders. They threaten political and economic dislocations here and in every other land where modern health conditions prevail.

When the Macy Foundation began its operations, the degenerative diseases, though they claimed a large share of the available medical care, received less attention from investigators than their importance justified. A great body of knowledge turned up in past decades of research had shown that the heart and circulatory system were so inextricably interrelated with such other systemic functions as those of the kidneys, the nervous system, musculature, and metabolism of the whole body that research into the degenerative processes must move along many fronts at once.

The Foundation's first step toward promotion of research in problems of aging was to undertake a survey of current investigations of arteriosclerosis, a disease that has afflicted mankind for thousands of years and still causes at least ten percent of the deaths in this country every year. Foundation officers consulted the Division of Medical Sciences of the National Research Council through its chairman, Dr. E. V. Cowdry, and asked the advice of leading investigators at home and abroad. The outcome was that Dr. Cowdry served as consultant and editor of a symposium to which a number of authorities contributed and which appeared in 1933 as *Arteriosclerosis: A Survey of the Problem* (Macmillan, New York).

Grants made by the Foundation to support chemical studies on cholesterol metabolism (of major import to understanding arteriosclerosis) under the direction of Professor Ludwig Aschoff in his institute in Freiburg, Germany (1931-1934), and to the College of Physicians and Surgeons, Columbia University (1933-1937) for work on cholesterol metabolism and its intermediary phases by Dr. Warren M. Sperry and Dr. Rudolf Schoenheimer, an associate of Aschoff's who came to the United States in 1933, produced important knowledge and techniques, such as the improved micromethod of Schoenheimer and Sperry for determining the amount of free and combined cholesterol in the blood.

Between the spring of 1931 and the end of 1934, the Foundation made grants to ten universities and research institutions for investigations on cholesterol metabolism, tissue growth, the role of blood supply to vessel walls, calcium metabolism, tissue changes in the kidney and liver, and for chemical, morphological, and experimental studies of arteriosclerosis.

In the course of his studies of cholesterol metabolism at Columbia University, Dr. Schoenheimer, in collaboration with Dr. Harold C. Urey, then Associate Professor of Chemistry at Columbia, developed a method of synthesizing organic substances in which part of the hydrogen was replaced by deuterium, or "heavy hydrogen." This use of heavy isotopes for tagging fatty substances fed to experimental animals in the study of intermediary metabolism brought revolutionary new knowledge to light. Instead of being static and inert after being laid down by the organism, as had been previously supposed, protein and fat tissues were seen to be extremely active, with constant interchange of molecules between these tissues and the fluids that surround them. Throughout the world today, rapid advances in the understanding of basic biochemical processes have been made possible by the work of Dr. Schoenheimer, which the Foundation supported from 1933 to 1941.

Research conducted in the past two or three decades gives strong indication that arteriosclerosis is a metabolic disorder related to the biosynthesis, transport, and metabolism of fatty substances. A relation between lipid metabolism and endocrine function has been demonstrated by studies of human patients and by animal experiments. The problem continues to offer a challenge to multidiscipline effort.

As the relation of arterial degeneration and vascular hypertension to kidney function, blood chemistry, capillary circulation, hormonal regulation, nutrition, and other aspects of body

81

function became more and more apparent, the Foundation extended its support to many related investigations in this country and abroad. Many of them are described in earlier Foundation reports (1937, 1941, 1950), and the obvious relation between a number of research projects described elsewhere in this report and problems of aging will be readily seen.

Dr. Cowdry, after his survey of arteriosclerosis, embarked upon a study of the broader aspects of aging. In 1937, with Foundation support, he undertook the preparation of a monograph on the subject, with a selected group of scientists in various fields to contribute to the study. In the summer of that year the Foundation arranged a two-day conference of the contributors Dr. Cowdry had chosen, at Falmouth, Massachusetts. Under joint sponsorship of the Union of American Biological Societies and the National Research Council, some twenty specialists in botany, genetics, entymology, nutrition, several branches of medical science and practice, psychology, anthropology, vital statistics, and philosophy met to bring their various data and points of view to discussion of the topic. The first edition of Dr. Cowdry's book* appeared in 1939, with a second edition in 1942 and a third in 1952.

A research program that has been supported by the Foundation over a long period is that conducted by the Committee on Research on Aging of the Department of Pathology, College of Physicians and Surgeons, Columbia University. Under the direction of Dr. Henry S. Simms, Assistant Professor of Biochemistry, two projects have been going on with Foundation assistance almost continuously since 1932: one concerned with research on deposition of fat in atherosclerosis, the other devoted to study of the factors that control longevity.

In the first, Dr. Simms and his associates have found that normal blood serum contains two substances that affect the

---

* Cowdry, Edmund V., ed, *Problems of Ageing, Biological and Medical Aspects*, The Williams & Wilkins Company, Baltimore. 1939. See also pages 14-15.

deposition of fat in the walls of blood vessels: lipfanogens, which are converted by living cells into visible fat deposits, and an antilipfanogen, part of which combines with lipfanogens or with cholesterol and inhibits fat deposition. The research group are at work on the isolation of antilipfanogen. By means of tissue culture methods, they are studying the role of the lipfanogens and antilipfanogen in causing atherosclerosis, a form of arteriosclerosis that is associated with diabetes, nephrosis, and coronary disease. Dr. Simms has been in contact with Dr. Ephraim Shorr, whose investigations of hypertension* bear relation to his work. Dr. Simms and Dr. Shorr were members of the Foundation's conference group on Problems of Aging.

In their studies of longevity, the Columbia group are concerned especially with the influence of age on the rate of accumulation of pathological lesions. They have statistical evidence, based on long-continued observations of a rat colony and comparative study of lesions in human tissues studied at autopsy, that age is an important factor in that rate; they are seeking to throw light upon the nature of the age factor.

Although studies of age changes in and regeneration of the nervous system have been made by a number of workers in the United States and other countries, it is a subject on which much experimental work is still needed. In the Department of Anatomy of the Bowman Gray School of Medicine, Wake Forest College, Winston-Salem, North Carolina, a team of three anatomists under the leadership of Dr. Warren Andrew is exploring the possibilities of regeneration of nerve tissue at various stages of individual and evolutionary development.

Though the power of regeneration is widely distributed in the tissues of lower vertebrates, until recently it has been believed to exist in the nerve tissue only in the embryological stages of those animals. Results of experiments have now suggested, however, that under proper conditions regeneration of cells of the central nervous system in fully developed mammals

* See pages 130-132.

and even in man may be possible. Using strains of pedigreed mice and observing them at ages that correspond to late middle age and senility in man, Dr. Andrew and his associates are making cytological studies of cells of different portions of the nervous system and the changes that occur in them with aging.

In the second phase of their investigation, the group will examine cells of brain, spinal cord, and the sympathetic nervous system of which the axone or nerve fibre has been severed. They hope to find out whether these cells, stimulated by the injury, will be rejuvenated, a process that would be indicated by regression of the signs of aging and the reappearance of structures characteristic of young cells.

The Macy Foundation made a three-year grant in 1953 for the support of this project. Dr. Andrew is a member of the Foundation's conference group on Diseases of the Connective Tissues.

The Foundation has contributed from time to time to support of the work of the Columbia University (College of Physicians and Surgeons) and the New York University College of Medicine research divisions of the Goldwater Memorial Hospital on Welfare Island. In 1951 it made five-year grants to both units to enable them to continue their investigations when New York City funds were curtailed. The Columbia University division has paid special attention to dietary factors in human hypertension and experimental arteriosclerosis in dogs. Its studies have included work on non-tuberculous bronchial pulmonary diseases, the rheumatic diseases, gout, renal diseases, and gastric physiology. The research program of Dr. Henry S. Simms and his associates has been correlated with the work of this group. The New York University division has been studying changes in body composition with advancing age, chronic diseases of the lung and of the liver, and problems of water retention.

As older persons become more numerous in our populace, the number of sufferers from chronic illness and of those who require major surgical operations in late life correspondingly increase. It is, therefore, important to understand the metabolic disturbances occasioned by these ordeals so that patients may be protected and helped to recover.

At the Yale University School of Medicine, investigators in the Department of Surgery under the leadership of Dr. Mark A. Hayes, Associate Professor of Surgery, are conducting biochemical and metabolic studies of adaptation and failure of adaptation to injury, operation, and serious illness. They are concerned chiefly with the functional interrelationships between the thyroid and the adrenocortical glands in their response to injury. Other studies are being made to evaluate the role of the parathyroid and pituitary-gonadotropic hormones and to find ways of correcting metabolic defects resulting from trauma. The Macy Foundation made a five-year grant in 1953 for the support of the project.

The importance of the psychological component in chronic illness has long been recognized by physicians. The Foundation in 1941 assisted a two-day conference on mental health in later maturity held in Washington by the Unit on Gerontology, National Institute of Health. The group's discussions brought out the fact that, contrary to popular belief, older persons with emotional and psychosomatic difficulties respond well to psychotherapeutic measures, and that understanding of psychosomatic mechanisms is as important for the practice of geriatrics as for all other branches of medicine.*

As the problem of care for the chronically ill becomes greater, it is ever more necessary to take full advantage of the preventive and rehabilitative potentialities of high morale and strong motivation toward recovery. During the last war clinical psychologists, in co-operation with psychiatrists, worked out new and better methods for evaluating the nature and intensity of the psychological component in illness,

---

* The proceedings of the conference were published as *Mental Health in Later Maturity*, Federal Security Agency, United States Public Health Service, Supplement No 168 to the *Public Health Reports*, Washington, 1942

methods that were used effectively by the military services and have been used since in Veterans Administration hospitals. They are too rarely adopted in civilian medical care.

In the southwestern part of the United States, where climate and medical service combine to produce attractive retreats for the chronically ill, the need for better co-ordination of health facilities for this large class of sufferers has been recognized by a number of physicians and efforts have been made to face the problem realistically. One such effort was a four-day conference organized by the Medical Branch of the University of Texas, with assistance and joint sponsorship by the Macy Foundation, and held at Galveston March 28-31, 1954. Thirty participants from the fields of medicine, surgery, psychiatry, clinical psychology, medical education, and medical administration discussed the subject of "Medical and Psychological Teamwork in the Care of the Chronically Ill." The co-chairmen were Dr. W. Paul Holbrook of Tucson, Arizona, an internist and chairman of the Foundation's conference group on Diseases of the Connective Tissues, and Dr. Molly R. Harrower, clinical psychologist of New York, who some years ago made modifications of the Rorschach method under Foundation support. The sessions followed the informal pattern of the Foundation conferences. The group divided into three study sections for intensive consideration of three aspects of the main subject: administration, training, and research, presenting reports to the whole conference for general discussion. The report of the conference was published in the fall of 1954.*

Since the Foundation began to make grants for research in aging and organized its conference group on Problems of Aging,† there have been developments of public and private character in the field and profound changes in attitude toward

---

* Harrower, Molly, ed., "Medical and Psychological Teamwork in the Care of the Chronically Ill," *Texas Reports on Biology and Medicine*, 1954, *12*, No. 3, 561-794.

† See pages 14-15, 82; *Twentieth Anniversary Review of the Josiah Macy, Jr. Foundation*, 33-34, 36.

the older citizens of the nation. Members of the conference group have been leaders in governmental activities such as the creation of the Unit on Gerontology within the Division of Physiology of the National Institutes of Health and the Section on Gerontology of the National Heart Institute, and many conferences, studies, and programs of research carried out by government agencies. They have also led in the organization of national and international congresses on gerontology. Officers of the Foundation have served as advisers to several government agencies concerned with problems of aging. The founding of the Gerontological Society in 1945 and the establishment of its official publication, the *Journal of Gerontology*, the following year, with Foundation support for five years,* were outgrowths of the conference group's activity. In fact, every one of the incorporators of the society had participated in the conference program.

In the 1950's, the problem of the elderly citizen has grown according to earlier prophecies, and the public has become more alive to it. There is greater awareness on the part of industrial management, business leaders, employers in all fields, and individuals in other age groups that a healthy, active person should not be tossed into a stagnating discard on reaching any arbitrarily set age, but must be given opportunities for a useful life, for his own sake and for that of the community.

---

* By the end of 1954, the *Journal of Gerontology* had more than doubled its subscriptions and had become self-supporting.

# THE INDIVIDUAL AND THE GROUP


MENTAL HEALTH is often described as a state of "feeling comfortable" about oneself and about one's relationships with others. From the individual's first group experience, his membership in the mother-baby twosome, throughout his life, his relationships with the members of the groups of which he inevitably forms part are a measure of his mental health.

Pursuing Mrs. Ladd's ideal of "the wholesome unity of mind and body," the Foundation has from its first years supported projects directed toward acquiring knowledge about the emotional nature of human beings and ways to help individuals learn to live harmoniously with others. Among those projects were studies of marriage and family relationships, adult education with reference to personality adjustment, improvement of social work education, and emotional factors and conflicts associated with delinquency. Studies of personality development in children (see p. 77), conferences and studies concerned with the psychological aspects of aging (see pp. 85-86), and much of the research falling generally in the category of psychosomatic problems are so closely related to the field of mental health that it is impossible to separate the areas with sharp lines.

## Comparative Studies of Animal Behavior

The study of animal behavior throws light upon problems in human psychology in much the same way that experiments on animals have contributed to the development of scientific medicine for the past six or seven decades. Psychologists have derived clues to understanding of human psychobiological processes from carefully controlled experiments performed on animals. Rats, dogs, cats, sheep, and goats have been observed in situations prepared to elicit certain responses; data from the experiments, analyzed and interpreted, are profitably applied to the study of human behavior.

In Europe during the past twenty years the study of animal behavior has received stimulation and new orientation from the thought and research of a Viennese psychiatrist and psychologist, Konrad Z. Lorenz, and his pupils, who call themselves ethologists — i.e., students of the relation of organisms to their environments. The ethologists have combined the experimental method of the laboratory with observation of animals in their natural habitats, performing their functions in normal parent-child relationships, in mating, fighting, and other forms of social behavior. Ethology is a union of natural history and experimental psychology, with new understanding of instinctive (unlearned) behavior brought about by the work of Dr. Lorenz and his pupils to illuminate principles long accepted by both naturalists and psychologists.

In the 1930's the Foundation supported two projects of pioneer value in the field of ethology: studies of the neurological and endocrinological basis of social habits in lower vertebrates directed by Dr. G. Kingsley Noble in the laboratory of experimental biology of the American Museum of Natural History, and the investigations of the growth of the nervous system and the early development of embryonic behavior in amphibia and other vertebrates by Dr. George E. Coghill.

Dr. Noble's investigations produced an important body of new information on the functions of the endocrine glands and of the sense organs and of the influence of hormone activities upon the development of behavior patterns in lower vertebrates. Dr. Coghill believed that the study of the *development* of behavior, resolving a mass of details into a science, should do for the understanding of behavior what study of embryology had done for understanding of anatomy. The anatomical and biological investigations he pursued through some four decades brought to scientists in many fields new knowledge of the development of the nervous system and the relation of that

90

development to the establishment of adult behavior patterns. The principles he enunciated as a result of meticulous observations contributed fundamentally to the biological interpretation of psychological problems.*

In 1937, Dr. Noble drew the attention of the Foundation's officers to the work of one of Europe's most promising students of animal behavior by showing them the manuscript of an English translation of Dr. Konrad Z. Lorenz's paper, "The Companion in the Environment of the Bird," an essay full of important observations on the relation of instinctive behavior to learned behavior. The Foundation had copies of the translation sent to a number of psychiatrists, psychologists, neurologists, and others in this country to whose work it could contribute.

In January, 1953, the Medical Director of the Foundation served as chairman of the first meeting of the World Health Organization's Study Group on the Psychobiological Development of the Child held in Geneva. One of the members of the group was Dr. Lorenz. Dr. Fremont-Smith was so strongly impressed with the high scientific quality of Dr. Lorenz's investigations and their potential value in studies of human social behavior that he visited Dr. Lorenz's laboratory in Germany later that year. Through this renewal of a contact first tenuously established sixteen years before, the Foundation seized the opportunity to assist a work of great promise.

Dr. Lorenz, an Austrian physician with training in zoology and psychology as well as medicine, for more than twenty years has devoted himself to comparative studies of behavior, particularly social behavior, in animals. He is now recognized as the founder of the European school of ethology. Since 1950, he has worked at the Max Planck Institute for Ethology† in Buldern, Westphalia, Germany. Here, with a

---

* Herrick, C. Judson, *George Ellett Coghill, Naturalist and Philosopher*, University of Chicago Press, Chicago, 1949.
† Formerly known as the Research Office for Ethology of the Max Planck Institute for Marine Biology.

staff of six assistants and his wife, who is a physician too, Dr. Lorenz has studied many forms of animal life from fish to mammals, though his most widely known observations have been those of birds. He has taken groups of birds, fish, and other small creatures into his household, sacrificing comfort and privacy so that he might observe them for months and years. For birds, he has provided a great degree of freedom, while maintaining conditions that permitted close watching. A case history method that Dr. Lorenz has developed and applied to his animal studies enables him to record manifestations of social relationships in his subjects with remarkable detail and acuity. His techniques, notable for their simplicity and thoroughness, have brought forth important discoveries.

Early in his animal studies Dr. Lorenz discovered that innate movements have relation to the evolution of the species just as do parts of the body — claws, beak, bones, etc. This led him to study the comparative morphology of movement, looking for the characteristics in a species that could help in reconstructing evolution. His studies extended to examination of behavior patterns and their survival value to the individual animal and to the species. Dr. Lorenz has proved to his own satisfaction, and to that of many others, the existence of instinctive, or unlearned, movements and has done much to clarify distinctions between those movements and learned behavior.

Expression of emotion and communication between members of a species are accomplished, Dr. Lorenz finds, by means of expressive movements and vocalization. Careful observation and analysis have enabled him to interpret much of that communication and even, in certain ways, to participate in it himself.

The theory by which Dr. Lorenz has perhaps most interested and influenced other investigators of animal behavior is that of innate releasing mechanisms and the responses they set in motion. Studying birds during the first few hours after hatching, he has been able to call forth the feeding response by presenting the baby birds with models that resembled the

92

parent bird only in shape and color of the bill. He has identified many stimuli in the actions of parent birds that evoke specific behavior responses in fledglings. He is convinced that many special organs, color markings, and characteristic movements have developed through evolution to serve as releasers of certain behavior in others of the same species. Thus inheritance (instinct) and environment (external stimuli) work together to produce behavior patterns.

As his studies reveal more about the relation of innate behavior patterns to evolution, Dr. Lorenz hopes to find out more and more about the evolutionary process and about its recapitulation in the development of the embryo during gestation.

The Foundation made a three-year grant beginning in January, 1954, to support Dr. Lorenz's investigations.

In the fall of 1954, Dr. Lorenz came to the United States to deliver the Messenger Lectures at Cornell University, the Dunham Lectures at Harvard Medical School, and others in institutions whose interests touch his own.

The experimental studies of animal behavior conducted by Dr. Howard S. Liddell at Cornell University since 1924 received support from the Foundation from 1937 to 1943.* They were concerned in that period with the physiological effects of experimentally induced neurotic behavior in animals and the relation of metabolism and thyroid function to maturation and adjustment. Dr. Liddell's ultimate goal is better understanding of the biological basis of psychological trauma. For the last seven years he and his associates have been investigating the problem of vulnerability of newborn and aged animals to environmental stress. In the laboratories of Cornell's Behavior Farm they have applied stressful conditioning to sheep and goats at various stages in the life span. They have succeeded in conditioning animals within five hours of birth and at the advanced age of ten years.

---

* *Twentieth Anniversary Review of the Josiah Macy, Jr. Foundation*, New York, 1950, 47-48.

Having noted the effect upon laboratory animals of the presence of a friendly human being during experiments, Dr. Liddell is studying the relationships of animals to one another and to man, especially the influence of maternal protection upon young animals. By laboratory experiments carried out with his colony of goats, Dr. Liddell, a pupil of Pavlov, has shown unmistakably that the mother's presence exerts a protective influence with lasting effect. Goats three weeks old were subjected to stressful conditioning for an hour a day for fifty days, some with the mother present, others without. The unprotected goats suffered the equivalent of psychic traumata; the others did not. Two years later, with no intervening laboratory experience, both groups were given daily two-hour stress periods in the conditioning laboratory. All of the previously unprotected goats soon showed signs of emotional disturbance; the maternally protected animals were unperturbed.

Research of the kind Dr. Liddell has been directing for thirty years, based on daily observation of experimentally controlled behavior of the same animals for periods of years, has great potential value for the clinical sciences. Dr. Liddell has had opportunity to compare human neurotic behavior with that of his laboratory animals. In the fall of 1952, he studied the emotional reactions of soldiers in Korea, observing that the signs of approaching breakdown in men long exposed to combat danger were closely similar to those heralding the emotional breakdown of animals subjected to prolonged anxiety stress.

Dr. Liddell and his associates have found usually that the experimental neuroses they have created in laboratory animals were truly chronic, that they affected the animals' behavior in barn and pasture quite as much as in the laboratory, but that they did not appear to shorten the animals' lives. In these respects the laboratory-produced neuroses correspond to certain psychoneuroses in man. New studies to be carried out in the Cornell laboratories will explore the role of the endocrine glands in increasing an animal's tolerance of environmental

94

stress and the possible benefit of hormones of the adrenal cortex and of the pituitary gland in treatment of neuroses.

Dr. Liddell has kept in touch with Dr. Lorenz and Dr. John Bowlby, whose studies of human infant-mother relationships at the Tavistock Clinic, London, have paralleled those of Dr. Liddell in animals.* One of Dr. Liddell's colleagues, Dr. Helen Blauvelt, has made studies of the mother-offspring relationship with goats. She has separated mother goats from their kids immediately after birth and noted the effect upon the mother-baby relationship after reunion and the degree and nature of disturbance produced in the kid by the separation. Dr. Lorenz has called Dr. Blauvelt's work a remarkable combination of the approach and method of the American and European schools of psychology and ethology.

The Foundation resumed support of Dr. Liddell's project with a five-year grant beginning in July, 1954, at the termination of assistance formerly given by the National Institute of Mental Health, United States Public Health Service.

### Conference on Group Processes

During September, 1954, the first meeting of a new Macy Foundation conference group was held in Ithaca, New York. The study of group processes is the object of this conference. At the five-day meeting that inaugurated its course, there were thirteen members from the fields of psychology, psychiatry, physiology, zoology, sociology, and anthropology, with seventeen guests representing the same disciplines and neuropathology, biology, and biochemistry, and the two leaders of the European school of ethology — Dr. Lorenz and Dr. Niko Tinbergen of Oxford University. Dr. Howard S. Liddell served as chairman, and Dr. Donald H. Barron, who is also receiving Macy Foundation support for his research on gestation, was among the members.

The conference brought together the proponents of two schools of thought — the American experimental psychologists

---

See pages 96-98.

and the European ethologists — with persons concerned with the application of knowledge of animal behavior to problems of human behavior, both normal and abnormal. Their frank discussions brought into the open first the differences, then the similarities in their approaches to the understanding of behavior of animals and men, and led to a genuine communication and appreciation between individuals and groups that had previously thought themselves in well nigh irreconcilable opposition.

## Separation of Child from Mother

Research into causes of mental illness, delinquency, and various forms of personality disturbances has adduced abundant evidence that traumatic experiences occurring in the first years of life are at the base of much later trouble. Disruption of the mother-child relationship for even a short period in early life may have deep effect upon the developing personality, possibly interfering with the child's capacity to form friendly, confident relationships with others in later years. Inability to establish and maintain stable co-operative relationships is a central feature of many forms of mental ill health. In recent decades most of the work of psychologists and psychiatrists on the emotional and social development of children has centered on the mother-child relationship, with revelation of much knowledge that has pointed the way to remedy for emotional disturbances in children and adults. There is still much to be learned in this wide area.

In London Dr. John Bowlby, Director of the Child Guidance Department of the Tavistock Clinic and consultant in mental health to the World Health Organization, has been studying the effects on personality development of separation of young children from their mothers. He has made direct observations of children two years old and younger during necessary periods in a hospital and has continued his observations in the children's homes after reunion with their parents. He has also studied a group of older children who had been patients in a tuberculosis sanitarium for varying periods in their first four years. Results of his studies have been reported in a number of publications. His monograph "Maternal Care and Mental Health," published by the World Health Organization in 1952, is believed to have had much to do with recent changes in child care programs in many parts of the world, including the United States. Dr. Bowlby wishes to pursue long-range studies to clarify further the understanding of needs of infants and young children and to determine how they may be met when separation from the mother is unavoidable.

Although many children are grossly and immediately disturbed by early separation, others go through the experience relatively unscathed. It is important to know what is the reason for this. Under what conditions can separation be more or less harmful? Such variables as the age of the child at the time, the length of the separation, the nature of the separation environment, the character of the relation with a mother substitute, experiences during the period, the nature of the mother-child relationship before and after separation are essential components of the problem.

Dr. Bowlby and his colleagues (a psychiatric social worker and three psychologists) hope to broaden their studies to include other aspects of the mother-child relationship in the early years. They will apply the data coming out of their observations to formulation of social programs, such as measures designed to prevent separations and to mitigate the adverse effects of those that cannot be avoided.

The Macy Foundation made a three-year grant, beginning in January, 1954, to the support of Dr. Bowlby's project, which receives support also from the International Children's Centre in Paris, the European Division of the World Health Organization, the Elmgrant Trust of London, and the Central Middlesex Group Hospital Management Committee, also of London.

The science of ethology has made important contributions to the study of human development, and no doubt will make more. Application of Dr. Lorenz's principle of innate releaser mechanisms set off by sign stimuli as the basis of complex social behavior of birds and fish and of techniques developed by Dr. Lorenz and Dr. Tinbergen to the study of social behavior of human beings promises to be of great value. Dr. Bowlby has been in contact with Dr. Lorenz for several years.

## Communication in Schizophrenia

Although depressing statistics furnished by state and federal agencies for years have shown mental illness to be the nation's biggest public health problem, less money is devoted to research into causes and treatment of mental disability than to research in any other major field of human illness. The Foundation has made grants toward the support of many studies of mental illness and its prevention which have been described in preceding chapters because of their relation to the subject areas of those chapters. In addition, the Foundation has aided studies of the effect of goal-directed interest (zest) upon the physiology of fatigue made by Dr. Warren S. McCulloch and Dr. Franz Alexander at the University of Illinois, Illinois Neuropsychiatric Institute, and studies of carbohydrate metabolism in mental illness, particularly schizophrenia, by Dr. McCulloch, Dr. Alexander, Dr. L. J. Meduna, and Dr. F. J. Gerty also at the Illinois Neuropsychiatric Institute from 1944 to 1947.

Among young adults, the major cause of commitment to mental hospitals is schizophrenia. There is great need for better understanding of the dreamlike state in which the schizophrenic patient exists, out of contact with reality and unable to communicate with others.

The anthropologist Dr. Gregory Bateson, through studies of the paradoxes of communication, has become especially interested in applying the insights he has gained from observation of communication among primitive people to the problems of schizophrenic failure of communication, a failure which, Dr. Bateson notes, includes the non-verbal signals by which the normal person supplements verbal expressions, classifying them as truth or fantasy, literal or figurative speech. Dr. Bateson works with psychiatrists and psychologists on the staff of the Veterans Administration Hospital at Palo Alto, under the guidance of the Research Committee of the Hospital and a committee of the faculty of Stanford University. In this project he will analyze recorded interviews between doctor and patient, between patient and patient, and between normal adults and children. He will develop experimental situations to bring out the contrast between normal communication and the broken communication of the schizophrenic. He and his associates at the Hospital and in the Department of Sociology and Anthropology of Stanford University are making a new approach to the description, theory, and psychotherapy of schizophrenia. The Foundation made a grant for the support of his study in the fall of 1954.

Dr. Bateson was a member of the Foundation's conference group on Cybernetics.

### Human Relations

Mrs. Ladd's injunction to her trustees to assist especially projects that call for the integration of biological, medical, and social sciences has been the central theme of the Foundation's activities throughout its two and a half decades, unifying all its interests so that with slightly shifting emphasis through the years that theme is still dominant. Many subject areas in which the Foundation has supported efforts, such as studies of psychosomatic interrelationships, improvement of social work education, use of adult education in personality adjustment, exploration of emotional factors in the learning process, personality development in children, consideration of the role of religion in illness and health, impinge upon the great area of human relations.

The four-day conference on clinical approaches to problems of human relations that the Foundation held in the summer of 1936* was an early venture in bringing representatives of medicine and the social sciences, with psychiatry as a unifying

---

' See pages 13-14.

discipline, to the consideration of biological and social studies of man's relations with his fellows. The conference program and the many ad hoc conferences organized by the Foundation, serving as experiments in inter-personal and inter-discipline communication, make their contributions to knowledge of human behavior in social relationships.

In the fall of 1946, informal discussions between Foundation officials and the Director General of Foreign Service in the United States Department of State led to a request from the Department that the Foundation conduct a series of informal round-table conferences on human relations in which participants would be a select group of Department personnel. Six of these conferences were held under the chairmanship of Dr. John M. Murray, Clinical Professor of Psychiatry at the Boston University School of Medicine and formerly chief consultant in neuropsychiatry to the Army Air Forces. Representatives of clinical psychology and cultural anthropology co-operated. Twenty-four members of the Department of State and the Foreign Service staffs joined in the attempt to find ways in which the insights of psychiatry and other social sciences could be made useful in the selection and placement of personnel and, in fact, in all the work of the Department.

## International Congress on Mental Health

Soon after the end of the last world war, persons and organizations in many parts of the world who had been active in the mental health professions, some as members of the International Committee for Mental Hygiene and others who had worked only within their own nations, felt the need of re-establishing contact with their colleagues in a truly international undertaking. The result was the holding of the International Congress on Mental Health in London in August, 1948. Nearly two years were spent in preparation for the meeting, under the direction of an organizing group in London. In the United States, the International Committee for Mental Hygiene, long inactive because of the war, sponsored the

Congress and organized the participation of the mental health professions in this country.

The program of the Congress, built around the theme "Mental Health and World Citizenship," was planned to be the outgrowth of the discussions of preparatory commissions — inter-discipline groups of workers in the mental health field — organized in all the participating countries. Some 350 such commissions with a total membership of more than four thousand men and women in twenty-seven countries worked on various phases of the Congress theme for several months in advance of the occasion and sent to London the reports of their considerations.

An International Preparatory Commission, a group of carefully chosen experts in psychiatry, psychology, sociology, anthropology, and other related professions, spent two weeks in a quiet, rural English setting before the Congress to discuss the reports of the local commissions and to draw up recommendations for action by the Congress. The statement* prepared by the Commission was fundamental for the deliberations of the Congress and has been useful to workers in the mental health field since then.

The Foundation contributed to the expenses of the Congress and to the work of the organizing committees in England and in the United States.

### The World Federation for Mental Health

Since 1945, the deterioration of international friendships that seemed to promise so much during the war and the increase of national sensitivity in many parts of the world have led men everywhere to a sober understanding of the need for nations to learn to get along together. The decade just closing has seen the creation of structures upon which international co-operation can be built. The United Nations

---

* *Mental Health and World Citizenship, a statement prepared for the International Congress on Mental Health, London, 1948,* World Federation for Mental Health, London, 1948.

and the many specialized intergovernmental agencies affiliated with it provide mechanisms through which governments may work toward peace.

To supplement the United Nations agencies composed of representatives of national governments, there are the international voluntary organizations serving the same function as do voluntary agencies at the national, state, or local level, such as Parent-Teachers Associations, for example. The international organizations stimulate, criticize, and co-operate with governmental agencies; sometimes they initiate pilot studies which, if they prove useful, are later taken over and supported by governmental bodies. The United Nations has recognized the need for the non-governmental agencies of special purpose by giving them consultative status.

An agency of this kind, the World Federation for Mental Health, was organized at the International Congress on Mental Health in London in 1948. Its interests are centered on human relations within all groups from the family to the family of nations, on promotion of the highest possible level of mental health among all peoples and nations. It has consultative status with the World Health Organization, the United Nations Educational, Scientific, and Cultural Organization, and the United Nations Children's Fund, and working relations with the Economic and Social Council of the United Nations. It works with national governments and international voluntary organizations whose programs touch upon mental health.

Members of the Federation are national or other organizations whose whole or partial purpose is the promotion of mental health and good human relations or the study of problems in this area. The founder members were the national mental health societies that had been affiliated with the International Committee for Mental Hygiene, the predecessor body that led in the formation of the Federation. In 1954, the Federation had eighty-six member associations in forty-one countries and several transnational associations. Individuals belong as associates.

The annual meetings of the Federation, attended by delegates and members of member associations, are held in a different country each year to stimulate interest in mental health work in different regions. Every three or four years the annual meeting coincides with an international congress on mental health organized by the national mental health society of the host country in co-operation and joint sponsorship with the Federation.

The World Federation came into being out of the conviction of interested persons in many countries that there was need to combine the insights into human behavior and human relations that have come from psychiatry and from all the other social sciences, notably education, psychology, sociology, and cultural anthropology. In the Federation's activities all the social science and health professions are on an equal basis. Their knowledge and skills are jointly brought to bear upon problems of the relations of human beings to one another, upon efforts to understand and deal with the social malaise currently afflicting the world at every level. Multiprofessional teamwork has long been used by hospital out-patient departments, school-community projects, programs for prevention of delinquency, etc. The same kind of teamwork is needed at the international level, and the international team will need especially to draw upon the resources of the sociologist and the cultural anthropologist, because they have made studies of the large groups and the conflicts among them.

The Federation encourages research and improvement of standards of training in mental health professions; collects and disseminates information of use in the field; holds conferences and congresses; sends consultants into the field; promotes liaison between member associations and the United Nations; and publishes a quarterly bulletin, *World Mental Health.* An activity that the Federation hopes to develop still further is the teaching seminar, such as the one held in Chichester, England, in the summer of 1952. With financial help from

WHO, UNESCO, the United States Public Health Service, the International Children's Center of Paris, and private sources, the seminar's faculty of twenty-three leaders in medical and social sciences drawn from France, Great Britain, and the United States and participants from thirty countries devoted three weeks to comparative study of the methods of rearing children during the first two years of life in the cultures of France, Great Britain, and the United States.* Similar institutes have been asked for in other parts of the world.

In addition to its long-range goal of helping to achieve international understanding, without which all other human ambitions seem futile, the Federation has a short-range goal; the furtherance of mental health activities at various local levels. Members and personnel realize that much work must be accomplished on this short-range program before they can hope to go far toward the more distant goal.

The Foundation, through its aid to the Congress of 1948, helped in the organization of the World Federation for Mental Health and made grants for the support of its program from 1949 through 1952. A number of special projects of the Federation have received Foundation assistance.

In the winter of 1954-1955, Dr. John R. Rees, Director of the Federation, and Dr. Fremont-Smith (President for 1954-1955) made a journey to a number of countries in Asia and Africa to establish contacts and seek ways in which the organization may extend its activities in those regions.

### Health and Human Relations in Germany

The relation of Germany to the Western democracies since the end of the war in 1945 has presented one of the most urgent, complex, baffling, and challenging problems of modern

---

* Staniland, Alan, "The Chichester Seminar on Mental Health and Infant Development," *Bulletin of the World Federation for Mental Health,* 1952, 4 (November), 168-171. A report of the seminar is to be published in the United States by Basic Books, Inc., and in England by Routledge & Kegan Paul, Ltd.

times. The allied occupation authorities found reconstruction of the life of the German people as demanding a need as the rebuilding of war-demolished structures. Just as slums of bombed-out cities could be replaced with well-planned, efficient new buildings, so Germans could make use of new insights and concepts in reconstituting their services for health, education, and social work. They needed material help, and they needed encouragement from their neighbors in the rebuilding of their moral and spiritual lives, salvaging what was good in their culture, casting out what was bad. An opportunity to share in a co-operative attack upon German problems by medicine and other social sciences appealed irresistibly to the Macy Foundation.

Dr. John R. Rees of London, Director of the World Federation for Mental Health, had heard a number of separate reports of studies made in Germany by experts working under government and private auspices, all in isolation from one another. He had also read the report of the Conference of Consultants on Services to Children in Germany called by the Children's Bureau in Washington in the fall of 1949. Dr. Rees suggested that a conference of officials and experts in education, community activities, health and welfare services in Germany would be helpful to the High Commissioners for Western Germany. By the spring of 1950, Dr. Rees' suggestion had won adherents and had taken form. At the request of the heads of the Children's Bureau (Federal Security Agency, now the Department of Health, Education, and Welfare) and of the National Institute of Mental Health (United States Public Health Service), and with their co-operation, the Foundation convened a five-day conference at Princeton, New Jersey, June 26-30, 1950. Participants were men and women with recent field experience in Western Germany, representatives of government agencies most closely concerned with German problems, a few experts from Great Britain and France, and a few Germans, the whole group limited to approximately thirty-five. The Department of State and the Office of the High Commissioner for Western Germany gave moral support and sent representatives to the gathering. The disciplines represented in the group were psychiatry, psychology, social work, cultural anthropology, and education. Fully two-thirds of the members were from private organizations or engaged in private practice of their professions; government officials participated as individuals. In every respect, the conference was unofficial. Its purpose was to help with the integration, analysis, and development of ideas and experiences. Any suggestion that the group might wish to impose the results of its thinking upon another nation was carefully avoided.

The five days of living in a quiet inn, removed from city pressures and distractions, of working with informality and friendliness in plenary sessions and in small groups brought about an understanding among persons of widely diverse cultural and professional backgrounds such as might not have been reached in months of ordinary professional contact. The four Germans present recorded the encouragement they took home from Princeton, growing out of the warmth of the conference association, the awareness — surprising to them all — that Americans wanted to help, not to direct, their efforts toward rehabilitation. Surprising, too, was the discovery that Americans had human relations problems not greatly unlike their own, and that Germans could help as well as be helped. Discussions had repeatedly shown that many German problems were universal, that ways of solving them could be applied elsewhere. Specific recommendations for action in Germany came out of the meeting, but all agreed that the living and working together was the unforgettable feature of the experience.

The report of the Princeton conference,* published in English, German, and French, appeared in time for use of par-

---

* *Health and Human Relations in Germany, Report of a Conference on Problems of Health and Human Relations in Germany, Nassau Tavern, Princeton, N. J., June 26-30, 1950,* The Josiah Macy, Jr. Foundation, New York, 1950.

ticipants in the White House Conference on Children and Youth in December, 1950. All three versions have been widely circulated in the United States and abroad.

One of the recommendations of the Princeton conference was that another be held immediately after the White House Conference to take advantage of the presence in the United States of Germans who came for that event and others here under the aegis of the Department of State. The Foundation gladly undertook the second conference, held at Williamsburg, Virginia, December 10-15, 1950. Here fourteen German psychiatrists, psychologists, social workers, teachers, youth leaders, only one of whom had been at Princeton, met with twenty-one Americans of equally varied professions, most of whom had been at Princeton, to continue the discussions and to carry further the programs suggested in the report of the earlier meeting. Great Britain and France again were represented. Dr. Rees was chairman, as he had been at Princeton.

The second conference began with some carry-over of fellowship from Princeton, but with obvious hesitation and withdrawal on the part of most of the German members, to whom the occasion was unprecedented and therefore full of uncertainty. Some passages of the Princeton report, which all had just read, aroused resentment in sensitive minds. There were emotional barriers to be surmounted before a working rapport could be reached. In amazingly short time, the good will of all members, their common purpose, the friendly atmosphere in which they worked together from day to day led to understanding and removed all vestiges of suspicion and doubt. The Williamsburg conference ended with the same achievement of friendly relations firmly established as had the one at Princeton.

Germans at Williamsburg frequently expressed the wish to have a third conference held in their own country. A recommendation to that effect was part of the program for future

107

activity adopted by the conference.* In the spring of 1951 a group of Germans who had attended one or both of the American conferences met in Frankfurt with representatives of the United States High Commission for Germany, Dr. Rees, and Dr. Fremont-Smith. The Germans asked the World Federation for Mental Health and the Foundation jointly to sponsor a conference in Germany in the summer of that year. They believed that a multiprofessional conference conducted on the Macy Foundation plan would give impetus to a movement that Germans could continue and expand. The request accorded with the policy of the United States to withdraw control gradually and to return responsibility for rehabilitation to the German people; therefore, the suggestion received the same warm support of the Department of State and the Office of the High Commission as had the two preceding conferences.

The third conference on Health and Human Relations in Germany met in a quiet country inn, the rest home of the Railroad Workers Union, at Hiddesen, near Detmold, North Rhine-Westphalia, August 2-7, 1951. The forty men and women who gathered under the joint chairmanship of Dr. Rees, Dr. Fremont-Smith, and Dr. Werner Villinger, Director of the Neuropsychiatric Clinic of the University of Marburg, represented 16 professions and seven nations. Twenty were Germans, of whom seven had been at either Princeton or Williamsburg. All the non-Germans had been concerned in some direct, personal way with German life in recent years.

To the Germans who had not attended the earlier conferences, a Macy Foundation kind of meeting was so new an experience that some preparation was needed. A German committee began work as soon as the time and place had been settled. Dr. Muriel W. Brown, of the United States Office of Education and a consultant to the World Federation for Mental

---

* *Health and Human Relations in Germany, Report of the Second Conference on Problems of Health and Human Relations in Germany, The Williamsburg Lodge, Williamsburg, Virginia, December 10-15, 1950*, The Josiah Macy, Jr. Foundation, New York, 1950, 27.

Health, who had had much to do with planning the preceding conferences, spent a month in Germany before the conference, helping in its organization.

When the participants assembled, they organized the conference, divided into four small work groups to consider the major areas into which questions selected in plenary session fell, fixed hours of work for the small groups and for the conference as a whole, etc. The conference was assured of complete freedom to follow its own subject development; there was no desire to limit discussion to continuance of those begun at Princeton or Williamsburg. A Swedish philosopher, a Dutch psychiatrist, and an American psychoanalyst gave informal addresses at plenary sessions, designed to evoke free discussion of subjects within the conference theme. In all its sessions the conference probed deep into the causes of tensions complicating human relations in Germany.

Again the conference plan worked well. Men and women of widely different training and professional experience and from countries that had lately been enemies talked frankly together of their problems, learning how basically similar their problems were, and how much they could help one another toward solutions. University professors and others whose age and attainments gave them professional eminence and young workers in youth movements and other social groups learned to listen to one another as colleagues. Respect, trust, and a strong *esprit de corps* quickly grew up among them. Except for the few veterans of Princeton and Williamsburg, it was a revolutionary experience. It could surprise no one who was there that it made a profound and lasting impression on all who shared it.

The chief recommendations of the Hiddesen conference were directed toward establishing a mental health movement in Germany.* It was to be a movement growing from community activities serving the needs of people, helping them to under-

* *Health and Human Relations, Report of a Conference . . . held at Hiddesen . . . August 2-7, 1951,* The Blakiston Company, New York, 1953.

stand and to solve problems in their daily lives. The conference made plans for fostering the movement in many ways. An interim committee of six was appointed to serve until a permanent liaison committee should replace it. Dr. Brown, with assistance from the Educational Exchanges Service of the Department of State and the Foundation, worked for seven months as a consultant for the Hiddesen committee and for the World Federation for Mental Health, studying existing mental health facilities in Germany and ways by which they could be helped.

In May, 1953, representatives of the local groups with which Dr. Brown and the Hiddesen committee had been working met in a conference at Haus Schwalbach, Bad Schwalbach, near Wiesbaden, Germany, to plan further co-operation. This is reported to have been a highly successful meeting. The group established close working relations and formed a liaison committee to continue their communication.

The revived interest in mental health activities in Germany, in which the three conferences have unquestionably played a part, has led to the formation of four mental health associations in West Germany now affiliated with the World Federation for Mental Health.

The Foundation's role in the three German conferences has been a peculiarly satisfying experience. The meetings have shown that the conference technique evolved for use by small multiprofessional groups of American scientists has value in multinational undertakings, that in fact the conference may prove to be an effective tool in the human relations field in and among nations. The three conferences on German problems confirmed the observations made repeatedly in the Foundation's continuing conference groups. In the meetings of American specialists at first one feels varying degrees of anxiety, even of apprehension; hesitation or volubility may indicate a defensive attitude, a possessive feeling toward one's special knowledge, a resistance to the data and hypotheses of

110

other disciplines. In the international group there are these feelings with the added barriers of language difficulties and cultural and political differences sometimes of near inflammability. As the conference proceeds, barriers come down and tensions relax among participants in spite of divergent backgrounds. Germans who attended the Princeton, Williamsburg, and Hiddesen conferences have said that the process, painful to many of them, through which they established communication with colleagues from the allied nations was possible only because they had been able to bring out and talk through the emotional blocks and basic differences that at first divided them.

The Foundation's association with the Department of State in this effort was especially rewarding. The interest of the Department's Office of German Public Affairs in the series of conferences and the subsequent work in mental health activities in Germany reveals a new concept in government policy. As Dr. Kellermann, then Director of the Office, expressed it at the Hiddesen conference* there is now a realization that contact between nations means contact between peoples; that success in dealing with other governments requires supplementing work done on the diplomatic level with intergroup and interpersonal work among the people for whom governments are responsible.

### The White House Conference on Children and Youth

The Midcentury White House Conference on Children and Youth, December 3-7, 1950, was the fifth in a series of decennial conferences on child welfare and development begun by President Theodore Roosevelt in 1909. The organizers chose as their central theme two questions for which the conference would try to find at least partial answers: "How can children be helped to develop the mental, emotional, and spiritual qualities essential for individual happiness and responsible citizen-

---

* *Health and Human Relations* (Hiddesen Conference), 147-148

111

ship?" and "What physical, economic, and social conditions are necessary to this development?" Two years of preparation by professional workers and laymen laid the foundation for the conference sessions. The Macy Foundation, with its continuing interest in development of the healthy personality, welcomed the opportunity to co-operate in pre- and post-conference activities.

The assistance given by the Foundation before the conference took two forms: a grant toward the budget of the Technical Committee on Fact-Finding, and co-operation by the Foundation's conference group on Infancy and Childhood.

Members of the conference group were participants in various phases of the White House Conference, two as members of the National Committee appointed by President Truman and three as members of the Technical Committee on Fact-Finding. At the request of the organizers of the White House Conference, the Foundation convened two special meetings of the Infancy and Childhood group in June and July of 1950 to prepare source material for the use of the Fact-Finding Committee. In addition, the group devoted one day of its regular meeting in March to the same purpose. Four members of the group prepared special reports on topics suggested by the Fact-Finding Committee and presented them for discussion at the three meetings. The four reports, with accompanying discussion, were distributed as preprints to the leaders of the White House Conference discussion groups. The unedited transactions of the Infancy and Childhood conferences were made available to the White House Conference, and the Foundation's *Symposium on the Healthy Personality,** containing three of the four special reports, was published in time for the use of discussion group leaders and participants.

---

* *Problems of Infancy and Childhood, Transactions of the Fourth Conference,
March 6-7, 1950,* The Josiah Macy, Jr. Foundation, New York, 1951
*Symposium on the Healthy Personality, Transactions of Special Meetings of
Conference on Infancy and Childhood, June 8-9 and July 3-4, 1950,* The
Josiah Macy, Jr Foundation, New York, 1950

Interagency Conference on Children

The Interdepartmental Committee on Children and Youth was organized in 1948 at the request of President Truman to help federal agencies co-ordinate and reinforce their activities. It included representatives of the Departments of Agriculture, Interior, Justice, Defense, and Labor, and various bureaus whose work affects the well-being of children and youth. The committee was active in preparation for the White House Conference.

In 1951, the vice-chairman of the Committee, Katharine F. Lenroot, Chief of the Children's Bureau, asked the Macy Foundation to hold a conference like those devoted to human relations problems in Germany, this one to help the agencies represented in the Committee to apply the findings of the White House Conference to their programs related to young people. Besides members of the Committee, Miss Lenroot and her associates wished to have consultants from professions concerned with mental health invited to the conference.

Nineteen members and associate members of the Interdepartmental Committee, four government resource consultants, and eleven non-governmental consultants — psychiatrists, psychologists, sociologists, social workers, physicians — gathered in the quiet setting at Princeton that had served the first German group so well. They conferred for five days in September. Previous meetings of the Interdepartmental Committee had been of the conventional type, with agenda, speakers, and discussion. Few members had ever worked closely together; few were really acquainted with one another, for all were members of large government departments and agencies of widely different purpose. Here, in the informal, spontaneous, and democratic conference setting, they brought their various knowledge and experience to bear on such topics as the development of responsible, mature adults; the strengthening of the family unit; the more effective use of manpower, especially in the young adult group; the prevention of waste of

113

human resources from psychosomatic disorders, emotional and mental illness, and other forms of social maladjustment. Following the usual Macy Foundation pattern for conferences of this size and duration, the group planned its own agenda, divided into small working parties, and used the consultants' special knowledge to supplement their own technical equipment.

The report of the conference* was widely circulated among government and private agencies interested in personality development in children and adults.

## Children's Bureau Conferences

Dr. Martha M. Eliot, who succeeded Miss Lenroot as Chief of the Children's Bureau and vice-chairman of the Interdepartmental Committee on Children and Youth, attended the Princeton conference and was impressed with its results. Among participants in her own agency and in others, she observed that the enthusiasm developed in the conference continued, that there was an increased interest in finding ways to use the work of the White House Conference, and that the ability to work understandingly with persons from other agencies, of different training and experience, acquired in the five days of living and working in a group had been a gain that was not lost on the return to daily routine. Dr. Eliot and others in the Children's Bureau wished to give members of the Bureau's central and regional staffs an opportunity to have a similar experience.

The Foundation gladly engaged in another co-operative project with a government agency devoted to the development of wholesome human relations. There were four conferences in 1952 — two held in Washington (January 3-5 and February 18-20) for members of the staff in the capital; one in Princeton (March 24-28) for regional and field staff in the states east of

---

* *Healthy Personality Development in Children*, The Josiah Macy, Jr. Foundation, New York, 1952. Distributed by Health Publications Institute, Inc., at cost ($1 00), net proceeds given to the National Midcentury Committee for Children and Youth, Inc., to aid in follow-up work of the White House Conference.

the Mississippi; and one in Colorado Springs (April 22-26) for staff in the West. The Field Foundation joined in sponsorship of the series.

The four conferences for the first time applied the Macy Foundation conference method to the working of a federal bureau staff; hence the venture was something of a pilot study. A degree of continuity was maintained by having the same chairman for all four — Dr. Edward D. Greenwood, of the Menninger Foundation — and by having some of the same consultants at all four gatherings. Each group planned its own agenda and procedures, the later ones making such changes as they thought desirable after hearing of the experiences of their predecessors. It was another step in the development of the conference program, from which the Foundation as well as the participating agency benefited.

Other Conferences

The Macy Foundation has frequently joined the New York Academy of Medicine in sponsoring conferences devoted to questions of special interest to the medical and allied professions. Some of these meetings have been mentioned in chapters dealing with the subjects discussed by the groups.

In the fall of 1951, the Committee on Public Health Relations of the Academy, at the request of the New York City Commissioner of Health, the Director of Health Education of the City's Board of Education, the Chairman of the Committee on the Use of Narcotics among Teen-Age Youth of the Welfare Council of New York City, and the Chairman of the Citizens' Committee on Children of New York City, desired to hold two conferences on drug addiction in adolescents. The Foundation assisted both undertakings.

The first conference was held at the Academy in November, 1951. A larger group of physicians, pharmacologists, psychiatrists, lawyers, social workers, religious leaders, teachers, probation officers, a judge, representatives of city, state, and federal law enforcement agencies and of private welfare

115

organizations attended the second conference, a two-day meeting at the Academy in March, 1952. The proceedings of the two conferences were published in book form in 1953.*

The need to prepare for mobilization of official and voluntary resources for the prevention and control of panic in case of war or other calamity led the Academy to hold a one-day conference to discuss the subject of morale and panic on February 2, 1951. The New York State and City Departments of Health, the Office of Civil Defense, and other public and voluntary health organizations co-operated; the Foundation gave financial support and joint sponsorship. A second conference to carry the discussions further was held by the Academy, again with Foundation support, at Arden House, Harriman, New York, November 3-6, 1954.

---

* *Conferences on Drug Addiction Among Adolescents,* The Blakiston Company, New York, 1953.

# RESEARCH IN MEDICINE

MINDFUL of their donor's wish that the Foundation should "primarily devote its interest to the fundamental aspects of health, of sickness, and of methods for the relief of suffering," the Directors have from the first supported the work of investigators who were inquiring into the nature and function of organs and systems of the body. In the early years, when the financial depression reduced the available funds of many grant-giving agencies, the Foundation was able to assist projects formerly supported by other private or government sources. Throughout the years, the Directors have chosen to aid studies of which the results promised to be of value beyond their immediate scope and investigators who ventured into unexplored areas and those who developed new techniques in their efforts to probe the secrets of nature.

With attention always to the importance of integrating roles within the body as well as between the individual and his environment, the officers have paid special attention to research directed toward systemic factors, toward chemical interrelations among organs and systems involving the hormones, vitamins, and other chemical agents.

Two Foundation-aided investigators have exerted deep and far-reaching influence upon the thinking of biological and social scientists in this country and elsewhere. Dr. George E. Coghill's observations of animal life from earliest embryonic stages, from salamander to opossum, produced fundamental knowledge of the processes of growth, integration, and individuation of the organism.* In the monumental work *The Biological Basis of Individuality*† the pathologist Dr. Leo Loeb

---

\* See pages 72, 90-91.
† Loeb, Leo, *The Biological Basis of Individuality*, Charles C. Thomas, Springfield, Ill , 1945. A Foundation grant to Washington University School of Medicine in 1937 assisted completion of Dr. Loeb's experimentation and publication of the volume.

117

incorporated the results of nearly five decades of research upon central biological problems. Dr. Loeb's elucidation of the nature of the inherent individuality of every member of the higher forms of animal life has meaning for students of genetics, embryology, ontogeny and phylogeny, pathology and bacteriology, endocrinology — in fact, nearly every branch of the medical and social sciences.

## Endocrine Glands

In the first year of its activity, the Foundation began making grants in aid of studies of the endocrine glands and their influence upon body functions. In 1930-1931 there were grants to the University of Berlin for the investigations of Professor G. von Bergmann on hyperthyroidism and to Cornell University Medical College, Department of Physiology, for studies by Dr. Graham Lusk and others on the influence of the thyroid upon metabolism. Dr. Frederick P. Gay's research on endocrine influence upon experimental infection, conducted in the Department of Bacteriology of the College of Physicians and Surgeons, Columbia University, received Foundation assistance in 1931-1933.

Investigations of the structure and function of the pituitary gland, or hypophysis, by Dr. Harvey Cushing and Dr. Kenneth W. Thompson at the Yale University School of Medicine were assisted by Foundation grants from 1935 through 1938. The research of these two investigators was directed particularly to the question of the tolerance to injection of certain hormones which the organism develops and application of knowledge of this phenomenon to clinical procedures for neutralizing the influence of over-active glands. The two scientists also demonstrated that the level of cholesterol in the blood is influenced by the activity of the pituitary gland.

As part of its program of research on problems of aging, the Foundation in 1936 began giving assistance to the research of Dr. Lester R. Dragstedt, Department of Surgery, University of Chicago, on the relation of pancreatic hormones to lipid

118

metabolism and arteriosclerosis. Dr. Dragstedt discovered a new hormone of the pancreas — lipocaic, the fat-metabolizing hormone — and adduced evidence that it is truly an internal secretion of the pancreas. He and his associates studied the physiology of the hormone and its role in diabetes and arteriosclerosis. Through Foundation officers, Dr. Dragstedt was brought into contact with the work of Dr. Schoenheimer and Dr. Sperry at Columbia University and a member of the Chicago research team spent some time in the Columbia laboratory learning to apply the technique of labeling molecules with heavy isotopes to the study of fat and carbohydrate metabolism. The Chicago group also conducted experiments to determine the significance of epinephrine in the problem of essential hypertension. The Foundation continued to support Dr. Dragstedt's investigations for ten years.

In 1936, the Foundation began aiding an investigation of the correlation of the menstrual cycle with the cyclic changes in the epithelium of the vaginal mucosa being made by Dr. Ephraim Shorr, then Assistant Professor of Medicine in the Cornell University Medical College and Chief of the Endocrine Clinic of New York Hospital. Through the next four years, the study was a fruitful collaboration of the Departments of Internal Medicine, Anatomy, Psychiatry, Pathology, and Urology. Dr. Shorr and his associates worked out methods for studying disturbances in the menstrual cycle and the physiological and psychological aspects of hormonal insufficiency during the menopause. Their investigation produced an impressive body of knowledge of many factors involved in the menstrual cycle and of related endocrinological problems. The techniques the group developed are still the best known methods for learning whether the replacement of hormones in the menopause is adequate.

The hormones of the cortex of the adrenal gland have been the object of extensive research by biologists, biochemists, and other scientists for several decades. In 1930, Dr. Leonard G.

Rowntree at the Mayo Clinic treated patients suffering from Bright's disease with an extract from beef adrenal cortex developed by Dr. W. W. Swingle and Dr. J. J. Pfiffner of the Princeton University Biological Laboratory. The results were amazingly successful. Dr. Swingle and Dr. Pfiffner, after several years of research, had isolated a hormone then believed to be *the* hormone of the adrenal cortex. From 1930 through 1933, the Foundation supported studies by these two investigators that contributed much to the knowledge of the function of the adrenal cortex, the nature of the only hormone then known to be secreted by it, and the relation of that hormone to various body functions. In 1934, Dr. Pfiffner received a Foundation grant to continue research on the cortical hormone in the Department of Biochemistry of the College of Physicians and Surgeons, Columbia University. A study of the hormone in relation to surgical problems made by Dr. William DeW. Andrus in the Department of Surgery of the Cornell University Medical · College was assisted by the Foundation in 1933 and 1934.

Investigations of the interrelationship between the adrenal cortex and the gonads made under the direction of Dr. C. C. Little at the Roscoe B. Jackson Memorial Laboratory were supported by the Foundation in 1939 and 1940.

Recognizing the potential usefulness of knowledge about the adrenal cortex in studying problems of traumatic shock, resistance to infection, and physical effects of high altitude flying, the Foundation organized conferences dealing with these subjects early in the last war, even before the entrance of the United States into the conflict. The first was a conference held for the National Research Council at Yale University in May, 1941. The physiologists, biologists, physiological and biological chemists, psychologists, internists, and representatives of the armed forces who met for an intensive two-day session were interested chiefly in the relation of the adrenal cortex to problems of anoxia, of shock, and of nutrition. The Foundation held other conferences on the same general subject, with emphasis on war-time needs, during the early 1940's.

A number of studies of special war-time problems closely related to functions of the adrenal cortex were supported by the Foundation in the same years, such as that of the steroid hormones, particularly those of the adrenal cortex, in relation to the problems of fatigue and other forms of stress suffered by aviators, conducted by Dr. Hudson Hoagland and Dr. Gregory Pincus at Clark University and the Worcester Foundation for Experimental Biology; an investigation of the metabolism of steroids, especially those of the adrenal cortex, by use of stable isotopes, made by Dr. Rudolf Schoenheimer in the Department of Biochemistry of the College of Physicians and Surgeons, Columbia University; Dr. C. N. H. Long's studies of the endocrine and chemical factors, particularly the hormones of the adrenal cortex, associated with conditions of stress, made at the Yale University School of Medicine; the investigations of the mechanisms and prevention of exhaustion following shock-producing agents, with special reference to the adrenal cortex, made by Dr. Hans Selye, then Associate Professor of Histology in the Department of Anatomy of McGill University; Dr. Ephraim Shorr's important studies of the molecular structure of steroid hormones by means of the infra-red spectroscope, carried on at the Cornell University Medical College. The Foundation supported Dr. Shorr's project, the first application of this technique to the study of steroids, from 1942 to 1946. The possible relevance of these hormones to problems of shock and high altitude flying led the National Research Council to ask Dr. Shorr to co-ordinate all the war-time infra-red spectrographic studies in this area.

Cortisone, one of the most clinically useful hormones of the adrenal cortex, is released under the stimulation of the adrenocorticotropic hormone (ACTH), which is produced by the anterior lobe of the pituitary gland. In 1943, two groups of investigators working quite independently, one on the West Coast and the other in the East, published their achievements

121

in isolating and purifying the stimulating hormone: Dr. C. H. Li, working with Dr. Herbert M. Evans in the Institute of Experimental Biology of the University of California, and Dr. C. N. H. Long and his associates in the Department of Physiological Chemistry of the Yale University School of Medicine. A Foundation grant for two years in 1943 made it possible for Dr. Li to complete his studies when other support was no longer available. He has since prepared a fragment of the ACTH molecule that carries all the therapeutic value of ACTH in much smaller doses.

Under Dr. Long's supervision, with the assistance of a series of grants beginning in 1943 and continuing into 1948, Dr. Abraham White and Dr. Thomas F. Dougherty studied the effect of the adrenocorticotropic hormone on lymphoid tissue. They contributed highly important observations of the effects of the hormone, acting through the release of cortisone, upon the body's ability to resist infection. Their studies also threw new light upon the relation of the adrenal cortex to kidney function and high blood pressure.

At the New York University College of Medicine, Dr. Elaine P. Ralli conducted research on vitamins and nutrition with help from the Foundation for several years beginning in 1933. In 1939, Foundation officers encouraged her and her associates to carry their studies into the field of hormone activity, especially the hormone of the adrenal cortex. At this time the Foundation was assisting Dr. Agnes Fay Morgan, in the College of Agriculture, University of California, to study the possible role of a filtrate factor of the vitamin B complex in preventing premature senescence in rats. Dr. Morgan had discovered that elimination of this factor from the diet of young rats led to graying of the hair, atrophy of the cortex of the adrenal gland, and premature aging. Dr. Ralli thereupon initiated animal experiments and studies of human patients with insufficiency of the adrenal cortex to see whether the use of the vitamin B filtrate factor would bring about improvement.

122

The experiments conducted by the New York University team confirmed Dr. Morgan's observations that vitamin B filtrate was necessary for the integrity and normal functioning of the adrenal cortex in animals. Normal pigmentation of skin and fur in black rats, lost through deprivation of vitamin B filtrate factor, was restored by removal of the adrenal cortex. The experiments had opened a new approach to understanding of the relation between nutritional factors and the adrenal cortex and of pigment metabolism. The Foundation continued its aid to Dr. Ralli's work until 1945.

In 1950, Dr. Ralli and her associates had learned that rats would survive for long periods after complete removal of the adrenal glands if fed large amounts of pantothenate, which had previously been known as the filtrate factor. Several other factors of the B complex (folic acid, biotin, and $B_{12}$) also prolonged the survival time, but not to the extent that pantothenate did. These factors also increased the ability of rats to withstand cold stress, affording clear indication that effective adjustment of an animal to stress, normally a function of the adrenal cortex, can be improved by additions of specific vitamins to the diet. The importance of clinical application of these findings is obvious. The new knowledge came to light at a time when the country's military authorities were especially concerned with the physical capacity of men stationed in climates hard to adjust to, flying at ever higher altitudes, and subject to many kinds of stress. The Foundation made a three-year grant to Dr. Ralli's group in 1951 and renewed it for another three years in 1954.

Dr. Ralli's investigations have gone to the roots of the interaction between hormones and body cells. Recently she and her associates have directed special attention to the influence of the hormones of the anterior lobe of the pituitary gland upon the synthesis of serum proteins by the liver. They will continue their explorations of the basic interrelationships between the action of hormones and the nutritional state of body

123

cells, with the hope that they may be able to explain some of the changes occurring in disease.

A Foundation conference group on the adrenal cortex was organized in 1949, the year in which announcements of the dramatically successful clinical use of cortisone and ACTH aroused lively interest on the part of the public as well as the medical profession in these two and related substances and spurred scientists to make intensive search for sources of adequate supplies of the pituitary-adrenal hormones. Under the chairmanship of Dr. C. N. H. Long, a group representing physiology, biology, biophysics, physiological chemistry, internal medicine, and pharmacology met annually for the usual five-year sequence of two-day sessions. Several investigators whose work in the subject area the Foundation has assisted were members: Dr. C. H. Li, Dr. Gregory Pincus, Dr. Elaine P. Ralli, Dr. Hans Selye, and Dr. Abraham White. Other grantees participated in individual conferences as guests. Several members had attended one or more of the war-time conferences on adrenal cortex.

Because of their role in the regulation of many body functions, the pituitary-adrenal hormones are an essential component of studies aimed primarily at other special problems. Investigators whose work the Foundation is currently supporting on hypertension and kidney function, blood coagulation and fibrinolysis, cold injury, liver disease and protein malnutrition, and still other subjects include within their projects research into the effects of the secretions of the adrenal cortex upon the functions of the organ or system of their special interest.

### Heart and Circulation

The Foundation has assisted a number of studies of the heart and blood vessels by investigators who approached the subject from the disciplines of surgery, medicine, biochemistry, neurology, and others. Many of the projects were concerned with the effects of aging on the heart and blood vessels and, therefore, were actually part of the Foundation's program of study of the problems of aging. Investigations of high blood pressure are, of course, inseparable from the subject areas of aging and the circulatory system, but a separate discussion of them follows this section.

Among early grants were a series made to the New York Post-Graduate Medical School and Hospital, Department of Medicine, for studies of capillary circulation conducted for several years by Dr. Irving S. Wright and the staff of the hospital's clinic for diseases of the peripheral vascular system.

Dr. Robert L. Levy conducted studies of coronary disease and cardiac pain, working in the Department of Cardiology of Presbyterian Hospital and the Department of Medicine of the College of Physicians and Surgeons, Columbia University, with Foundation support from 1935 through 1941. He and his associates investigated the effect of reduction of oxygen content of the air breathed by the patient upon heart pain. Their work led to development of a clinical test, by means of induced anoxemia, for detection of coronary insufficiency. The test made possible studies of the effects of various drugs upon heart action. It also enabled investigators to follow the interference with coronary circulation in sclerosis of the coronary blood vessels and measure the development of new collateral circulation after a coronary thrombosis had taken place.

In the late 1930's, the Foundation aided two surgeons who made important contributions to advancement of surgery of the heart, a field then much in need of development. From 1935 through 1939, grants to the Pathological Institute of Western Reserve University School of Medicine supported the investigations of Dr. Claude S. Beck who, for some ten years, had been trying to find surgical methods of improving the failing blood supply to the heart muscle of patients suffering from coronary diseases. After long animal experimentation, by 1936 he was able to apply to human patients his new technique by which he provided a collateral blood supply to the myocardium sufficient to compensate at least in part for the loss of circulation through coronary arteries narrowed by arteriosclerosis. His achievement opened new possibilities for development of surgical therapy in cases of coronary thrombosis.

Dr. Beck collaborated with a colleague at Western Reserve, Dr. Victor C. Myers of the Department of Biochemistry, whose research on the creatine content of heart muscle the Foundation supported in 1934-1935. Dr. Myers made chemical studies of the heart muscles of experimental animals used in Dr. Beck's laboratory, with results beneficial to both projects.

As Dr. Beck continued his investigations, he was able to promote collateral circulation to the heart muscle by tissue grafts that allowed new blood vessels to grow into the heart from surrounding tissues. He gave attention to improving the mechanical factors interfering with the heart's action and to determining whether ligations of the coronary veins would improve circulation through the heart muscle.

In all such attempts as Dr. Beck's to supply blood collaterally to the heart, a major problem was that of oxygenation. Another surgeon, who fortunately was trained also in physiology, made a notable advance in the solution of this problem, enabling Dr. Beck to improve his operation for use on human patients and greatly enlarging the possibilities for cardiac surgery. Dr. John H. Gibbon, Jr., then in the Department of Surgery at the University of Pennsylvania School of Medicine, received grants from the Macy Foundation from 1937 through 1940 to assist his attempts to develop an apparatus that would provide artificial circulation for the heart and lungs of cats during operations on those organs. After much painstaking work, in which he was helped by engineers as well as medical and surgical colleagues, Dr. Gibbon perfected a machine that would take over the functions of heart and lungs through longer and longer periods. War service took Dr. Gibbon away from his project for some time, but a few years after his resumption of it his work led to an epoch-making operation on a human being for correction of a congenital heart defect.

126

The apparatus of his devising provided circulation of oxygenated blood through the patient's brain, enabling the surgeon to open the heart and operate in a bloodless field.

The Foundation contributed to the studies of neurogenic and hormonal influence on the cardiovascular system conducted by Dr. G. E. Hall in the Department of Medical Research of the Banting Institute, University of Toronto; Dr. Herrman L. Blumgart's investigation of the relation of clinical manifestations of coronary heart disease to pathological findings, with special reference to the development of collateral circulation, carried out in the Department of Medicine of the Harvard Medical School in 1939-1942; and, in 1942-1944, studies of circulatory collapse in infectious diseases under the direction of Dr. Blumgart and Dr. A. S. Freedberg, also at Harvard.

The intricate, perfectly-balanced system, developed through the process of evolution, which keeps the healthy mammal's blood in a fluid state and yet causes it to coagulate at the site of a vessel rupture resulting from injury or disease is still imperfectly understood.

One of the leading investigators in the field of blood coagulation, Dr. Tage Astrup, of the Biological Institute, Carlsberg Foundation, Copenhagen, has spent many years studying the agents in the blood that regulate the rate and reversibility of clot formation. In 1951, the Foundation made a two-year grant to the Carlsberg Foundation to supplement assistance received from a Danish scientific society for Dr. Astrup's work. At that time Dr. Astrup was especially interested in the relation between clotting and the alarm reaction, i.e., the mechanism by which pituitary and adrenal cortex hormones, secreted in response to stress situations, increase the rate of clotting. He had a group of young scientists working with him on the problem; a number of publications recorded the encouraging progress of their research.

As their studies of the fundamental mechanisms of blood coagulation advanced, Dr. Astrup and his associates found the

127

process to be far more complicated than they had previously supposed. They discovered a number of new components involved, some of which appear also in human urine and milk. They are now at work upon quantitative methods of estimating each component and studying all of them under physiological and pathological conditions. They are studying the activating and inhibitory principles in various tissues to learn the nature of their role in the development of the organism's capacity to reverse clotting. The group's investigations have already brought to light many important facts about clot formation and have increased understanding of its fundamental biochemistry. In their physiological studies of the process they have looked into the connection it has with rheumatic diseases and with immunology. They have worked also on the clinical use of anticoagulants such as heparin and dicoumarol to control too hasty clotting.

The Foundation continued support of Dr. Astrup's work through a period to end December 31, 1956. Financial assistance from Danish sources has been continued also.

In 1948, the first conference of the Macy Foundation group on Blood Clotting and Allied Problems was held. Dr. Astrup was among the participants. He reported on the investigations of his group at the Biological Institute and contributed to the group discussion. He found the meeting so helpful that he has kept in touch with the succeeding conferences. It was Dr. Astrup's suggestion that led the Foundation to make regular provision for at least one foreign guest at each conference instead of just taking advantage of the presence in this country of an investigator from abroad at the time of the conference.

## Hypertension

The many questions involved in understanding the mechanisms by which blood pressure is regulated have challenged investigators for years. In Belgium, the distinguished scientist, Professor Corneille Heymans, and his laboratory staff in the Department of Pharmacology of the University of Ghent had investigated the nervous regulation of circulation and respiration for some ten years when, in 1934, the Foundation undertook to assist their research. The group expanded their studies to include several aspects of the physiology of blood pressure control, with results that won for Professor Heymans the 1938 Nobel prize for physiology.

To study degenerative diseases of the blood vessels, investigators needed a method of producing in laboratory animals conditions similar to those found in man. A project supported by the Foundation for several years beginning in 1931 was the investigation of the relation between arterial hypertension and arterial degeneration conducted by a team of research workers under the direction of Dr. George R. Minot in the Department of Medicine of Harvard Medical School. The group explored several methods of inducing arterial hypertension in animals. By 1934, Dr. Soma Weiss and other members of the group were investigating the nature of vasopressor substances found in the urine and blood of patients with different types of hypertension as well as in healthy persons. As their studies turned up important data about the relation of diet to arteriosclerosis, Dr. Minot and his associates gave considerable attention to the role of vitamin deficiency in the causation of certain kinds of cardiovascular disturbances. From 1936 to 1938, the Foundation's assistance was given to this aspect of their studies.

Meanwhile, at the Western Reserve University School of Medicine Dr. Harry Goldblatt had been studying experimental hypertension for some time. In 1934, he announced success in producing high blood pressure in animals by clamping the renal artery so as to reduce the blood supply to the kidney.* His discovery gave stimulus and new direction to many investigators of the broad subject of hypertension.

At Vanderbilt University School of Medicine, Dr. Tinsley R. Harrison, Associate Professor of Medicine, who had been investigating various possible causes of hypertension, in 1936

---

* The Foundation contributed to Dr. Goldblatt's investigations of hypertension from 1937 through 1941

129

confirmed Dr. Goldblatt's discovery and conceived the idea that the kidney might contain a blood-pressure-raising substance that entered the circulation in greater quantity when the blood supply to that organ was decreased. From 1937 through 1939, the Foundation assisted Dr. Harrison's research into the nature and action of this substance.

In the course of studies of permeability of capillaries of amphibia and mammals, supported by the Foundation in 1939-1940,* Dr. Robert Chambers and Dr. Benjamin W. Zweifach of the Department of Biology of New York University devised an apparatus making possible new methods of observing the effects of various agents on circulation of the capillary bed. Recognition of the importance of their work for studies of shock in connection with military problems led to expansion of their research in this direction and the discovery of the presence of a "toxic" material in the blood of animals suffering from shock. Injection of rats with this material, partially isolated from the blood of animals in shock, produced shock-like changes in the rats' blood vessels. Further studies, in which blood taken from animals in the early stage and in the later, "irreversible," stage of shock following bleeding was injected into rats, produced evidence of a pressor substance present in the early stage and a depressor substance in the later stage. The Foundation continued support of the project, which was aided also by the National Research Council, through 1943. An important development of the findings of Dr. Chambers' group came about in another New York research institution.

In 1945, Dr. Ephraim Shorr and a group of colleagues at the Cornell University Medical College and New York Hospital were studying hypertension and shock, with the work of Dr. Goldblatt and the New York University team, and the chance observation of Dr. Paul György, as their point of departure.† With the aid of a grant from the Foundation beginning in

---

ʰ See pages 28-29.
† *Idem*

1946, and with Dr. Zweifach added to their number, the group began an expanded research program.

The basis of this investigation, as of Dr. Chambers', was the capillary bed, the system of minute vessels through which the cells of the body are nourished and relieved of their waste products. Medical scientists have known for many years that epinephrine, formed in the medulla of the adrenal gland, is one of the main factors controlling the flow of blood through the capillary bed. The research of Dr. Chambers and Dr. Zweifach and the later work of Dr. Shorr, Dr. Zweifach, and their associates threw new light on the control of capillary circulation. The significant fact about the pressor and depressor substances first demonstrated by the New York University group and confirmed by the Cornell University team is that the one accentuates the effects of epinephrine upon the capillary bed and the other decreases those effects.

Dr. Shorr and his associates found that the pressor substance, which they named VEM (vasoexcitor material), is produced in the kidney and the depressor, VDM (vasodepressor material), in the liver, both substances appearing in the blood only when the supply of oxygen to those organs is reduced. When an animal is bled, there is at first an outpouring of VEM from the kidneys; this maintains blood pressure and circulation through the capillary bed in spite of the loss of blood. If the bleeding is stopped shortly, the animal will recover. If bleeding lasts too long, the liver responds to the diminished blood and oxygen supply with an outpouring of VDM and the beneficial effects of VEM are lost. Unless blood is promptly restored by means of a transfusion, the irreversible stage of shock ensues.

VEM also appears in the blood of experimental animals in which hypertension has been induced by the Goldblatt method of partially shutting off the blood (and oxygen) supply to the kidney by means of a clamp, and in the common form of high blood pressure in man. This fact proves a real analogy between the human condition and that experimentally produced in

131

animals. VEM is present in eclampsia and is undoubtedly one of the important factors involved in human hypertension. Its chemical nature has not been identified.

By the use of triphenyl tetrazolium chloride as a stain, the Cornell group have demonstrated a derangement of the enzymes of the cells of the kidney tubules and of the adrenal cortex occurring in both experimental and human hypertension, further demonstrating the analogy between experimental and human high blood pressure.

VDM, produced in the liver in small quantities normally but in large amounts as soon as the oxygen supply is reduced, appears in the blood not only in shock, but also in a number of other conditions such as cirrhosis of the liver, nephrosis, and decompensated heart disease. It has been identified by Dr. Shorr and his associates as ferritin, the iron protein previously regarded only as the body's chief reservoir of iron. Ferritin has now been found to be implicated in the formation of hemoglobin and in the transport of iron across the placental barrier from mother to fetus.

This research program, supported by the Foundation continuously since 1946, is an example of a genuine multidiscipline approach to a medical problem. Members of the research team — physiologists, biochemists, organic chemists, and clinicians — work together, making clinical and laboratory studies of hospital patients suffering from hypertension and shock, laboratory studies of the clinical syndromes of hypertension and shock reproduced experimentally in animals, studies of derangements of enzyme systems within the cells of the experimental animals — derangements that underly the clinical phenomena, and partial identification of these enzyme changes in the cells of patients.

Dr. Paul Govaerts, one of the leaders of academic medicine in Europe, resumed the activities of his laboratory of experimental medicine at the University of Brussels as soon as he could after the liberation of his country from the German occupation. With two promising young men, one experienced in cardiology and the other in renal physiology, Dr. Govaerts began to rebuild his laboratory staff and to expand his research on function and diseases of the kidneys and the cardiovascular system. Within a short time he had put to work a number of physicians, biochemists, and other young investigators. In 1947, the Foundation began to support the work of Dr. Govaerts' laboratory at the University of Brussels.

One of the important early results of this research was the discovery of a new interrelationship between the adrenal cortex and the kidney in which a hormone from the adrenal cortex makes it possible for the kidney to conserve, in the blood, sugar that would otherwise be lost in the urine. Dr. Govaerts and his associates have made fundamental studies of the relation of renal function to hypertension, kidney disease, the influence of suprarenal hormones on kidney function, and related subjects. Their work is, of course, related to that of Dr. Shorr and his group. Contact between the two laboratories has been established to the benefit of both. Some of the young men working with Dr. Govaerts have spent periods in the United States, which has enabled them to introduce techniques developed here into the studies under way in the Brussels laboratory.

Investigations carried out under Dr. Govaerts' direction have confirmed by entirely different methods observations made in this country, notably by Dr. Shorr and his associates, that in the early stages of experimental hypertension the blood appears to contain a hypertensive substance which, once the high blood pressure has been well established, seems to disappear from the blood.

In 1953, the Foundation made a further two-year grant to the University of Brussels. The most recent publications from Dr. Govaerts' group record the progress of four studies: experimental studies of the mechanism of renal hypertension; investigation of the mechanism of protein excretion by the kidney; investigations concerning adrenal hormones; experiments

133

relating to the possibility of removing barbiturates from the blood by peritoneal lavage in cases of barbiturate poisoning.

The group brought together by Dr. Govaerts is recognized as one of the most productive in Europe. The Foundation is gratified to have had the opportunity to make it possible for Dr. Govaerts to re-establish the teaching and research center destroyed by war and to bring it to a high level of accomplishment.

A Foundation conference group on Factors Regulating Blood Pressure, under the chairmanship of Dr. Harry Goldblatt, held the first of five annual meetings in 1947. Dr. Shorr and Dr. Zweifach were among the members. Because of the many organs and systems involved in the etiology of high blood pressure, the group's discussions covered a wide range of physiological problems, with considerable attention given to renal function.

## Liver and Kidney Function

Research into the structure, function, and diseases of the liver and kidney is an inseparable part of investigations of the causes and treatment of high blood pressure and study of problems of aging. Some of the projects supported by the Foundation may be mentioned independently of these two areas, however.

In 1931, a grant to Stanford University assisted continuance of an investigation into the mechanism of hypertrophy and atrophy of the kidney which Dr. Thomas Addis had been conducting for several years.

In the same year, Dr. Addis and Dr. Jean Oliver, of the Department of Pathology of the Long Island College of Medicine, published a book, *The Renal Lesion in Bright's Disease.* A Foundation grant to the Long Island College of Medicine, also in 1931 and continued for a few years, aided Dr. Oliver's studies of the anatomical and functional features of experimental nephritis in the frog. Dr. Oliver's special interest was in the architecture of the kidney in the later stages of vascular and renal disease, notably in Bright's disease. Using old and simple methods, he undertook a study of the abnormal kidney that was an important new departure in research upon that organ. He worked out a method of dissecting under the microscope the individual nephrons, the microscopic physiological units of which there are a million in each kidney, thus providing the first understandable explanation of what goes wrong in various kidney diseases.

With more Foundation assistance, Dr. Oliver published his monograph, *The Architecture of the Kidney in Chronic Bright's Disease*, in 1939 (Paul Hoeber, New York). It has become a classic of medical writing. Recognition of the importance of Dr. Oliver's work has come in many forms during the years. In 1953, he was appointed the first Distinguished Service Professor at the State University of New York College of Medicine.

Dr. I. S. Ravdin, Professor of Research Surgery and Director of the Laboratory of Research Surgery at the University of Pennsylvania School of Medicine, received Foundation assistance from 1934 to 1937 for his studies of the formation and fate of bile in health and disease and the relation of the gall bladder to biliary function. Foundation officers brought about contact between Dr. Ravdin and Dr. Rudolf Schoenheimer at the College of Physicians and Surgeons, Columbia University, to their mutual benefit, for both men and their associates approached common questions, such as the nature and action of cholesterol, from different points of view.

In the 1940's, Dr. DeWitt Stetten, Jr., a pupil of Dr. Rudolf Schoenheimer, used the technique of labeling fat molecules with isotopes of heavy hydrogen and nitrogen in studies of the intermediary metabolism of choline, colamine, and related compounds. Working in the Department of Biochemistry of the College of Physicians and Surgeons, Columbia University, with Foundation assistance from 1940 through 1947, Dr. Stetten learned new and important facts about fat metabolism and the mechanism of fatty infiltration of the liver that occurs in certain vitamin deficiency states. His research contributed toward understanding of the processes of fatty metabolism in the central nervous system as well as in the liver.

The Foundation is currently supporting two projects concerned with the liver and kidneys. In 1954, it made a three-year grant to the Johns Hopkins University School of Medicine for Dr. Allan L. Grafflin's research on the relation of structure and function in the cells of liver and kidney. Dr. Grafflin observes the living cells of those organs of frogs and mice under the ultra-violet microscope after injection of fluorescene to make them visible. He is particularly concerned with the consequence of inadequate oxygen supply to the liver, a condition that occurs in low blood pressure from traumatic and post-operative shock. He is using the same technique to gain a better understanding of the mechanism by which kidney cells remove impurities from the blood.

In the course of studies of radiation sickness for the Atomic Energy Commission, Dr. Paul F. Hahn, Director of the Cancer Research Laboratories of Meharry Medical College, found that dogs intravenously injected with radioactive gold developed severe injury of the liver where the gold accumulated. The observation suggested a new method of producing chronic and acute liver damage experimentally — useful to investigators because current methods did not bring uniform results. Determination of the maximum tolerance of dogs to internal irradiation and the influence of such factors as age, quantities and intervals of dosage, and effect of alteration of diet upon the response of the liver to irradiation are of fundamental importance in studying radiation injury caused by excessive exposure to x-rays or radioactive substances and in finding means of protection against such injury.

Dr. Hahn and Dr. H. E. Meng, of the Department of Physiology at Vanderbilt University School of Medicine, have undertaken a joint study of experimental cirrhosis of the liver induced by irradiation with radioactive gold. They have found

136

that young dogs – under twenty weeks old – are much more likely to develop liver injury from irradiation than are adult dogs. Experimental bleeding combined with irradiation hastens cirrhosis and ascites (accumulation of fluids in the abdominal cavity) in older animals. Dr. Hahn's studies have shown that the liver is capable of withstanding massive amounts of internal irradiation, a fact that has profound clinical significance in the treatment of many diseases, notably malignancies, with radioactive substances. Dr. Hahn is continuing studies to determine the role played by iron in cirrhosis resulting from irradiation.

Another phase of the project is concerned with the development of fatty liver. Dr. Meng has demonstrated that heparin, an anticoagulant produced in the liver, injected into dogs will prevent the accumulation of fat in the liver, a common result of diets high in fats but deficient in choline. He is investigating the effects of hormones on the production of fatty liver and upon transport and utilization of lipids. In collaboration with the Departments of Pediatrics and Pathology, he hopes to study the composition of liver of normal infants and of those with fatty changes. The Foundation assisted the co-operative investigation of Dr. Hahn and Dr. Meng from 1951 through 1954.

A group of investigators concerned with various aspects of liver injury met for the first time in the summer of 1943 and twice a year during the war. It became one of the longest-continued of the Foundation groups, holding its twelfth and last meeting in 1953. Among the members were several scientists whose work had been aided by the Foundation: Drs. Goldblatt, György, Shorr, and Stetten.

A conference group on Renal Function held its first session in 1949, with Dr. Grafflin and Dr. Oliver among the members.

A recently-formed conference group has a subject that concerns investigators working in a number of overlapping areas: Shock and Circulatory Homeostasis. Under the chairmanship

137

of Dr. Ephraim Shorr, it held its first meeting in 1951. Its immediate purpose was to revive the multidiscipline approach to problems of shock that had been so fruitful during the last great war, problems again made urgent because of the fighting in Korea. Members are concerned with shock in relation to surgery, circulation in general, the role of the kidney and liver in regulation of circulatory balance, permeability of membranes (especially the walls of capillaries), the role of the sympathetic nervous system, metabolic aspects of hemorrhagic and traumatic shock, shock phases of radiation injury, shock resulting from bacterial invasion, and other problems. There is, of course, much community of interest between this group and that on Factors Regulating Blood Pressure.

## Nutrition

Professor Albert Szent-Györgyi, the Hungarian biochemist and founder of the Institute of Medical Chemistry of the University of Szeged in Hungary, engaged Dr. Kast's interest in the early 1930's, when his identification of vitamin C and other biochemical studies won acclaim in many parts of the world. Dr. Szent-Györgyi and his colleagues were then devoting a great deal of thought to the problem of energy transfer, trying to find out how energy liberated in oxidation is transferred to other reactions. For three years, 1932-1934, the Foundation made grants to aid the work of this group on vitamins and cell oxidation. From 1935 to 1940, the Foundation's support was given entirely to the research on the mechanism of biological oxidation, the results of which won for Dr. Szent-Györgyi the Nobel prize for physiology and medicine in 1937.

During this period, Dr. Szent-Györgyi and his associates discovered that the rind of lemons and other citrus fruits contains another antiscorbutic substance in addition to vitamin C. Isolating this new chemical, Dr. Szent-Györgyi named it vitamin P, because of its effect upon the permeability of capillaries. He and his colleagues announced their discovery in the summer of 1936,* suggesting the use of the new vitamin in the treatment of septicemia and other infections. Dr. Szent-Györgyi's studies of vitamin P and the related group of flavonoids, continued during the years since his identification of vitamin C and since his emigration to the United States, have led to his recent discovery of flavonoids in the human thymus which may prove to play a vital role in the control of growth.

Dr. Szent-Györgyi has made an important contribution to the understanding of the mechanism of muscular excitation and contraction and of the conversion of chemical energy into mechanical energy in the living organism. The Foundation supported the early phases of this research at the University of Budapest in 1947-1948.

During the 1930's the Foundation aided a number of studies of the nature and therapeutic effects of vitamins. Notable among them was a study of the relation of vitamin A deficiency to diabetes mellitus made by Dr. Elaine P. Ralli at New York University College of Medicine under a grant made in 1931. A new grant in 1933 assisted Dr. Ralli in studying the relation of blood cholesterol and vitamin A. Later, 1938-1940, the Foundation supported Dr. Ralli's investigations of the human requirement of vitamin C and the effect of insulin on metabolism of vitamin C. In 1939, Dr. Ralli began her studies of the effect of vitamin B filtrate on the adrenal cortex described on pages 122-124.

Dr. George Wald, of the Harvard University Biological Laboratories, the first investigator to identify vitamin A in the retina, has made a series of brilliant contributions to the knowledge of the chemistry of the visual pigments and the mechanism of vision. In the late 1930's, he discovered a new photosensitive substance in the retinal cones of which he believed vitamin A

---

* Rusznyak, St., and Szent-Gyorgyi, A., "Vitamin P: Flavonols as Vitamins," *Nature*, 1936, *138*, 27 (July 4).

to be the precursor. In 1939, he began a new series of biochemical studies of human vitamin A deficiency in relation to night blindness and of carotenoid and vitamin A deficiency metabolism in the retina and other tissues. From that year to 1943, the Foundation assisted Dr. Wald's investigations. In 1941, he returned to fundamental studies of such matters as the comparative biochemistry of visual systems, cone photopigments and the chemistry of color vision, the chemistry of retinal pigments, and the synthesis of vitamin A. Dr. Wald's long-term work and special investigations he made in connection with war problems have been of basic importance to the subject of nutrition and to understanding of the chemistry of the eye.

There were grants also to the University of Copenhagen, Biochemistry Institute, for Dr. Henrik Dam's studies of the chemical, biological, and biochemical problems connected with vitamin K (1937-1939), and later a small grant to the Marine Biological Laboratories in Woods Hole for Dr. Dam's investigation of vitamin E deficiency; to the University of Cincinnati College of Medicine for a study of the use of nicotinic acid in the treatment of pellagra by Dr. T. D. Spies; to Cornell University Medical College for investigations of biotin metabolism in man by Dr. Theodore Oppel; to Harvard Medical School for a study of human requirements of thiamin and the metabolism of thiamin in normal and diseased states by Dr. Benjamin Alexander; to the University of Illinois for Dr. Ernst Gellhorn's studies of the effect of vitamins of the B group on resistance to anoxia and the role of the adrenal cortex in protecting the body against damage resulting from anoxia; to Oxford University for assistance to the Oxford Nutrition Survey, a war-time project carried out under the direction of Dr. Hugh Sinclair, with the support of the British Medical Research Council and the Ministry of Health, to determine the nutritional status and needs of the British people, especially in the industrial areas.

Throughout the tropical belt of the world a disease called kwashiorkor ("red boy" in a West African language) afflicts millions of persons, especially children between the ages of one and four. It is not a new disease, nor always confined to tropic regions in the past, having been observed in Europe and as recently as 1947-1948 in Hungary. Study of the condition in the tropics for many years was complicated by the importance attached to parasitic diseases there; even when it became clear that malnutrition was a major part of the cause, cases were frequently diagnosed as pellagra. Treatment based on this diagnosis, with large quantities of vitamins, particularly vitamin B, not only did not cure, but often proved lethal. Only when feedings of extra protein — quantities of steak and other meats — brought marked improvement of cases in Africa did the chief cause of the illness become apparent.

Kwashiorkor most frequently attacks infants within a few months after weaning. The child becomes markedly underweight, though his abdomen, legs, feet, or other parts of the body may be swollen; he is anemic, with wasted muscles, lacking in appetite, apathetic, peevish, and soon seriously ill. At a certain stage fat accumulates in the liver, though enlargement of the liver is not a constant sign. The symptom that gave the disease its name is a change in pigmentation. The tightly-curled hair of the healthy African child becomes coarse, straight, and dusty brown or red — in severe cases even flaxen. Dark-skinned patients lose color, especially around the mouth. The fatality among untreated cases is high, but there is always favorable response to treatment with a diet rich in protein. Untreated patients who survive are left with permanently damaged liver, pancreas, and perhaps other organs.

At the Macy Foundation's ninth conference on Liver Injury in 1950, Dr. J. N. P. Davies, Professor of Pathology in the Makerere College Medical School, Kampala, Uganda, described kwashiorkor and the clinical and investigative work he and his associates had done on it. By that time the disease had been reported in virtually all of Africa, Central and South America,

141

India, Assam, Indo-China, and Indonesia. The next year, at the tenth conference, Dr. Kenneth R. Hill, Professor of Pathology in the newly-founded University College of the West Indies, Jamaica, gave an account of liver disease in Jamaican children that corresponded in most respects with kwashiorkor.

In 1950, Professor Hill invited Dr. Paul György, Professor of Nutrition in Pediatrics in the University of Pennsylvania School of Medicine, and Dr. Joseph Stokes, Jr., Professor of Pediatrics at the University of Pennsylvania, to visit Jamaica. The two men were profoundly impressed with their observations of dietary deficiency conditions and resultant diseases practically unknown in the United States. The result of this visit was the initiation of a program of joint studies made under the direction of Professor Hill at the University College of the West Indies and at the University of Pennsylvania School under Dr. Gyorgy. The Foundation made a three-year grant to the University of Pennsylvania for support of the project in 1950 and renewed it for another three years in 1953.

Dr. György's studies soon suggested to him that the ailing Jamaican children were afflicted with a disease in which infection or toxic factors and dietary deficiency both were involved. He has traced the toxin, not yet isolated, to a tea brewed from two native plants and consumed in large quantities by children. The deficient item in diet, it is generally agreed, is the animal protein factor, the equivalent of vitamin $B_{12}$, which is essential for utilization of proteins and for the maintenance of normal liver function.

The observation that children begin to show signs of kwashiorkor soon after weaning, even though they may be getting more protein than they did when they were breast fed, puzzled investigators. Dr. György has shown that breast milk contains a factor, not yet identified, that protects infants against the illness, even though the milk contains insufficient protein for adequate nutrition. If Dr. György's early observations of this circumstance are confirmed, some vitamin or other

142

element in breast milk may prove useful in prevention and cure of this and other liver disturbances.

Dr. György has found also that fermentation of diet mixtures seriously deficient in protein may improve their biological value. He has the co-operation of the Food and Agriculture Organization and the World Health Organization in obtaining food mixtures from various parts of the world both before and after fermentation. Knowledge of the nature of the beneficial alteration caused by fermentation will be of help in improving deficient diets and may solve the economic problem of enabling inhabitants of under-developed regions to obtain the diet they need.

The Jamaican group has succeeded in showing the difference between the particular liver ailment that is common among children of the island and the usual form of protein malnutrition of which the chief characteristic is fatty liver. Only twenty percent of the liver cases in Jamaican children are classifiable as typical kwashiorkor. The eighty percent suffer from serous hepatosis. Both conditions are the result of low intake of protein, especially of animal protein.

Deficiency of protein in diet is responsible for a long list of diseases prevalent in the economically depressed areas of the tropics and for generally poor physique and low resistance to infection. Estimates of the numbers of inhabitants of the tropical and subtropical sections of the world who are or will be affected by liver injury resulting from protein malnutrition run into astronomical figures. Chronic protein deficiency, especially during the period of growth, may affect the body tissues and organs so severely as to make cure impossible. Prevention and protection of coming generations offers the best hope of reducing the ravages of this affliction.

The Food and Agriculture Organization and the World Health Organization have been concerned with protein malnutrition throughout the world for some years. When the Joint Expert Committee of the two organizations held its third meeting, at Fajara, Gambia, British West Africa, in the late fall of 1952, one of its recommendations was to hold a conference to consider the whole problem. Dr. Paul György, a member of the Joint Expert Committee and of the Foundation's group on Liver Injury, joined the heads of the nutrition divisions of the FAO and the WHO and others in planning the conference. Under the committee's auspices, twenty-six specialists in nutrition, biochemistry, physiology, pathology, pediatrics, internal medicine, and public health from India, Africa, Great Britain, Central and South America, Australia, and the United States met at the University College of the West Indies, Jamaica, November 2-6, 1953. The Foundation took an active part in planning and supporting the conference. Application of the Foundation's plan of informal round-table discussion proved effective in this multinational, multidiscipline group as it has many times before.*

In the fall of 1954, the planners of the Jamaica conference asked the Foundation to support another conference to pursue the work begun by the earlier one. Recognizing the incalculably great influence that the stamping out of kwashiorkor and similar disabilities could have upon the health, economy, and culture of a vast portion of the world, the Directors willingly agreed to assist and sponsor, jointly with the FAO and the WHO, a second conference on protein malnutrition, to be held in Princeton, New Jersey, in June, 1955. It will deal primarily with the qualitative and quantitative aspects of protein requirements in tropical areas, especially for children in the post-weaning period, and will plan research needed to determine those requirements.

### Nerve Impulse

Dr. David Nachmansohn, a German-trained physician and biochemist who came to the United States in 1939, had worked for many years on investigations of the nature of the nerve

---

* Waterlow, J. C., ed., *Protein Malnutrition, Proceedings of a Conference in Jamaica, (1953)*, University Press, Cambridge, England, 1955.

144

impulse. By 1942, when he was engaged in research in the Department of Neurology of the College of Physicians and Surgeons, Columbia University, and in the Neurological Institute, he had made important contributions to the understanding of the process of conduction of signals along the nerve fibre, both within the brain and in the peripheral nerves. From that year to 1948, the Foundation assisted Dr. Nachmansohn's studies of the mechanism of the transmission of the nerve impulse, a process that underlies every human activity, thought, or feeling.

Before Dr. Nachmansohn's research, two rival theories had been advanced in explanation of nerve impulse transmission: an electrical and a chemical theory. Dr. Nachmansohn, using the most delicate electrical measuring devices, made possible by discoveries in electronics, and the newest chemical tools, turned to studies of the electric eel, the goldfish, and even the squid as well as of higher vertebrates in his search for answers to the riddle.

The theory of transmission of nerve impulse worked out by Dr. Nachmansohn and his associates combines electrical and chemical phenomena. They have shown that the passage of the nerve impulse is associated with, and apparently depends upon, the sudden release of a chemical, acetylcholine, at the surface of the nerve fibre, and that the recovery of the fibre, so that it may be ready to transmit a second impulse, is in turn dependent upon the rapid destruction of acetylcholine by the enzyme cholinesterase. The nerve at rest is poised and ready for instant action, like a loaded rifle. Acetylcholine pulls the trigger to fire the impulse, and the enzyme cholinesterase, by removing acetylcholine, permits prompt reloading to take place, the whole process of firing and reloading requiring only three or four thousandths of a second. There is much that remains to be elucidated about this complicated and fundamental process. Dr. Nachmansohn's studies have had enormous practical value in pointing a direct approach to the development of new drugs that would accentuate or diminish nervous activity by stimulating or inhibiting the enzymes involved with nervous action.

In the early years of Dr. Nachmansohn's studies in the United States his observations and concepts were received with skepticism by other investigators because they ran counter to currently accepted views. His data are now widely recognized in this country and abroad as sound, well established, and highly illuminating. Agencies of the federal government have recently made substantial grants to support of Dr. Nachmansohn's expanded research program.

The Foundation's conference group on Nerve Impulse in its five meetings (1950-1954) brought together a number of specialists in neurology, biology, physiology, biophysics, biochemistry, zoology, anatomy, and other disciplines. In the uninhibited give-and-take of these small gatherings of investigators in a highly specialized subject area, as reported in the transactions, it is possible to follow the growth of understanding within the group, the clearer specification of differences of opinion and contradictions in data, and the emergence of new areas for investigation.

## Cold Injury

A war-time problem that has had the continued attention of scientists is the pathophysiology of cold injury. During the last great war, forces of many nations suffered devastatingly from exposure to severe cold, with much loss of limb resulting from faulty treatment. The engagement of United States troops in Korea and the establishment of defense bases in many cold regions spurred our scientists toward more investigation of the nature of the damage suffered by body tissues from exposure to cold, methods of preventing such injury, and therapy for unavoidable disability.

The Foundation, in co-operation with the medical branches of each of the nation's armed services, organized a conference group on Cold Injury in 1951. Most of the members and guests who attended the three meetings held up to the winter of 1954 had participated in military research programs on the subject; several were currently members of the military medical services. Canada and Great Britain were represented at all three meetings. Participants were selected from the fields of physiology, biophysics, internal medicine, pathology, surgery, climatology, and epidemiology.

The conference discussions dealt with the fundamental scientific aspects of cold injury and with clinical problems such as causative mechanisms of frostbite, lowered resistance to infection resulting from exposure to cold, and hypothermia — abnormally low body temperature — in which research had been interrupted by the war of 1941-1945 and which is of use in surgery, especially of the heart.

The Canadian Department of Defense invited the group to hold its third meeting at Fort Churchill, Manitoba, where the Department maintains a research laboratory. The Royal Canadian Air Force flew the members from Winnipeg to Fort Churchill. A number of Canadian scientists joined the regular members for the four-day meeting in February, 1954. Though holding a conference at so remote a spot in the cold season had seemed a formidable undertaking, it proved to be a highly successful one.

One of the members of the conference group, Dr. Steven M. Horvath, Professor of Physiology at the College of Medicine, State University of Iowa, has been investigating the response of human beings to exposure to cold, with Foundation support since 1951. Dr. Horvath and his associates have conducted experiments on animals and men. With a well-equipped cold chamber, they have observed the effects of sub-zero temperatures on medical students in good health; they have also used cold exposure with patients suffering from disturbances of circulation in the limbs. The tests of normal persons revealed a surprisingly wide variety in ability to withstand exposure to cold. Analysis of the physiological factors underlying such differences contributes much to the understanding of the body's adaptive mechanisms and of the failure of those mechanisms in certain circumstances. In his animal experiments, Dr. Horvath has been able to keep dogs at an internal body temperature of 24°C. (75°F.) for more than twenty-four hours with complete recovery upon rewarming.

Another member of the Cold Injury conference group is Dr. Janet Travell, Associate Professor of Clinical Pharmacology at the Cornell University Medical College, whose investigations of the mechanism of referred pain the Foundation has supported since 1951. Dr. Travell has mapped patterns of referred pain for most of the musculature of the body and several of the internal organs and has discovered new patterns of pain distribution, particularly of pain resulting from muscular injury and disease.

The investigations conducted by Dr. Travell and her associates have shown that both acute and chronic pain depend upon the integrity of a reverberatory circuit connecting certain newly-discovered "trigger points" in the skin and muscles or the affected organ and the central nervous system. Through clinical studies the group has demonstrated that procedures to block the trigger mechanisms, interrupting the pain cycle, will bring relief. Even transient interruption of the reverberatory circuits by injection of novocaine into muscle trigger points or by chilling skin trigger points with ethyl chloride spray will provide temporary and sometimes permanent relief of intractable pain. Such severe pain as that of coronary thrombosis has yielded to treatment with the ethyl chloride spray. The achievement of permanent relief of pain in cases of first and second degree burns has revealed the fact that such continuing pain depends upon self-sustaining cycles rather than upon local tissue damage.

Dr. Travell is continuing investigations into the nature of trigger areas in muscle structures, the interrelations of muscular trigger areas and visceral function, metabolic and nutritional factors in chronic muscular pain, and the effect of cold sprays (ethyl chloride and other materials) on the pain produced by burns and injury by cold. She is a member also of the Foundation's conference group on Connective Tissues.

In 1954, the Foundation made a three-year renewal of its grant for support of Dr. Travell's project, which is assisted also by the National Heart Institute, United States Public Health Service.

## Bone Physiology

The fundamental studies of physiology of bone conducted by Dr. Franklin C. McLean at the University of Chicago have had the interest and support of the Foundation through a long period. From 1933 through 1937, grants assisted his investigations of the metabolism of calcium and phosphorus and the physiochemical state of calcium in the blood and other body fluids. After a transition period in the late 1930's during which Dr. McLean was concerned chiefly with the blood-bone relationship, he and his associates enlarged their program to embrace many aspects of the physiology and biochemistry of bone. The Foundation assisted the program in 1940-1942, and resumed support of it after the war in 1946-1950.

In 1937, a recent science graduate of the University of Michigan came to Dr. McLean's laboratory for study before beginning his medical training. That was the beginning of a close and productive collaboration between Dr. McLean and Dr. Marshall R. Urist, now Assistant Clinical Professor of Surgery at the University of California in Los Angeles. The two investigators, though they have lived in the same city for only two of the intervening years, have jointly written a number of papers and a book entitled *Bone: An Introduction to the Physiology of Skeletal Tissue*, published by the University of Chicago Press in 1954, as the first of a new series – The Scientist's Library, *Biology and Medicine*.

In the years between 1943 and 1953, Dr. McLean and his

149

colleagues and investigators in other laboratories built up a considerable body of material about the physiology of bone. There was clear need for a synthesis of data and viewpoints on the subject. National recognition of the need took form in 1953 in the creation by the National Research Council of a Sub-committee on the Skeletal System. Dr. McLean and Dr. Urist are members of it.

The Foundation in 1953 made three-year grants to the University of Chicago and the University of California to support a collaborative project of Dr. McLean, whose emeritus status beginning that year enabled him to give his full time to research, and Dr. Urist. The two men are compiling a series of monographs on the physiology of bone. They will bring together the results of research never before collected in a related fashion. The authors' recently published work referred to above is a part of the project.

Both investigators are conducting research under the grants, too. Dr. McLean is investigating the role of induction in the growth and regeneration of bone; the nature of the local mechanism in calcification; the mechanism of resorption of bone; the role of hormones, vitamins, and enzymes in the physiology of bone; and, using tracer techniques, the formation of new bone under the influence of radioactive estrone.

Dr. Urist is studying the physiology, histophysiology, and histochemistry of bone formation and repair. He is observing particularly the process of bone formation in estrogen-treated animals and is using radioisotopes in the study of the physiology of bone transplantation.

Dr. McLean became a member of the Foundation's conference group on Metabolic Aspects of Convalescence in 1946; he was a member of the successor group on Metabolic Interrelations throughout its five years. The transactions of the meetings of these two groups furnish an important record of research in bone physiology during a period when great strides were made. Dr. McLean considers participation in the sessions of the two groups to have been an essential feature of his investigations.

## Tuberculosis

A safe, reliable vaccine against tuberculosis has eluded the pursuit of researchers since the beginning of the era of scientific medicine. Robert Koch followed his epoch-making discovery of the tubercle bacillus (1882) with another observation that threw light upon the nature of the organism. In 1891 he recorded that when a normal guinea pig was inoculated with a pure culture of live or dead tubercle bacilli, after ten to fourteen days at the site of the seemingly healed wound there appeared a firm nodule which formed an ulcer that persisted until the animal died. But if an animal previously infected with tuberculosis were similarly inoculated, the wound closed quickly, no nodule appeared, and after a day or two a shallow ulcer formed and quickly healed. Koch had rediscovered the phenomenon of hypersensitivity announced by Jenner in 1801. He had shown the existence of a state of acquired resistance to reinfection, and he had proved that the dead bacillus retains many important properties of the living.

For a long time investigators believed that hypersensitivity and acquired resistance were manifestations of a single phenomenon, that the former was the promotive factor in the latter. Further research, however, showed that there is no correlation between the intensity of hypersensitivity developed in immunized animals and their acquired resistance to subsequent infection. It followed that in the body of the dead tubercle bacillus there are two substances — one highly toxic, the cause of hypersensitivity, and the other protective. This explains the failure since Koch's time of efforts to produce a wholly acceptable vaccine.* The importance of separating the

---

* In 1924, the French scientists Calmette and Guérin introduced their strain of attenuated bacilli as a vaccine for human beings. Since then, great numbers of babies in various parts of the world have been protected by doses of the famous BCG. It carries, however, the potential danger of any vaccine containing live bacteria, i e., that the bacteria, multiplying within the body, may regain their virulence and produce the disease.

toxic and the protective substances from each other is readily apparent.

In 1939, a young Frenchwoman trained in physics and chemistry was working at the University of Paris and the Pasteur Institute, applying her physicochemical knowledge to research in microbiology. Turning her attention to the tubercle bacillus and using a simple paraffin oil extract of virulent tubercle bacilli, she was able to sensitize normal guinea pigs, the first successful sensitization of these animals by any but whole live or dead bacilli. Her work promised to shed light on fundamental problems in the understanding of the phenomenon of acquired resistance and the production of an immunizing agent. The Nazi occupation of Paris interrupted her work and sent her to New York, where she continued her investigations in the laboratories of the Department of Public Health and Preventive Medicine at Cornell University Medical College.

From 1942 to 1947, the Foundation made grants to Cornell University Medical College to assist the studies of Dr. Nine Choucroun. War conditions had given even greater urgency to work on prevention of tuberculosis. The incidence of the disease rose alarmingly in Europe and elsewhere as a result of troop movements and mass displacements of civilian groups.

In the fall of 1946, Dr. Choucroun returned to her native country. There she found that scientists were desperately in need of help as they struggled to recover from the occupation's damage to their morale and resources. With the warm endorsement of her former colleagues, Dr. Choucroun worked out a plan for co-operative investigations between the Cornell laboratories and the Centre National de la Recherche Scientifique. A renewed grant from the Foundation to the Cornell University Medical College in collaboration with the Centre National made it possible for Dr. Choucroun for several years to spend half of the year working at the Institut de Biologie Physico-Chimique in Paris and half in New York at the Cornell laboratories. In France she was able to recruit a group of brilliant young investigators in the fields of chemistry, immunochemistry, and pathology, and by means of small stipends and provision of essential apparatus, to make a considerable beginning in the reactivation of research in tuberculosis in France.

By 1950, the French government was contributing through the Centre National de la Recherche Scientifique to the cooperative program. In the spring of 1954, Dr. Choucroun returned permanently to France to continue and extend her studies there. The Foundation has made a grant to the Institut de Biologie to run until 1959, in decreasing annual amounts because of the growing support the French nation is making toward the project.

Dr. Choucroun's own work, starting with the paraffin oil extract, has resulted in the isolation from the tubercle bacillus of a carbohydrate — a lipopolysaccharide — capable of producing in guinea pigs and in man hypersensitivity to tuberculin and specific protective antibodies. It gives a precipitin reaction with blood serum of tuberculous patients, the only direct precipitin test for diagnosis of human tuberculosis. The extract may point the way to the best effective non-living vaccine against tuberculosis in man. Dr. Choucroun has already vaccinated persons from six months to twenty-two years of age, with resulting indication that antibodies have been produced in them. She has the collaboration of two French hospitals in developing the quantitative precipitin test and in verifying the results of vaccination with the lipopolysaccharide.

Dr. Choucroun's work is an example of the application of techniques from basic science disciplines to medical problems. Even if it should not reach the goal of certain prevention of tuberculosis, it would have laid the groundwork for new approaches of great potential value. It has already brought about mutually beneficial scientific collaboration between France and the United States.

JOSIAH MACY JR. FOUNDATION

## Corneal Basement Membrane

A highly specialized study with potentialities extending into other fields is that of Dr. Herbert M. Katzin, Associate Surgeon and Director of Research at the Manhattan Eye, Ear and Throat Hospital, and Dr. C. C. Teng, Research Associate at the Hospital, on a part of the eye. In 1953, these two investigators announced their identification of a basement membrane in the cornea distinguishable by staining methods from the corneal epithelium and Bowman's membrane.* They have continued morphological studies of the membrane and its role in maintenance of the fluid balance of the cornea. Their observations throw light upon the basic physiology of the cornea and upon such questions as the adhesion of the corneal epithelium to Bowman's membrane, the permeability of the cornea to drugs and chemicals.

Dr. Katzin and Dr. Teng are also investigating pathological changes in the basement membrane, using material from patients with diseased corneas. Their work will help improve means of preserving corneas in living state for tissue graft purposes. More far-reaching results may be expected from comparison of the basement membrane of the corneal epithelium with other basement membranes in such structures as the choroid plexus, the ciliary body, the kidney glomerulus, and others.

The Foundation made a three-year grant in 1954 to support the studies of Dr. Katzin and Dr. Teng.

## Purification of Allergens

A study of pollens that evoke symptoms of allergy now being pursued with Foundation assistance has a history dating back many years. In 1939, a grant to the Department of Anatomy, College of Physicians and Surgeons, Columbia University, assisted Dr. D. H. Moore, a physicist, to develop use of a new electrical method — electrophoresis — for isolation of

* Teng, C C., and Katzin, H. M., "The Basement Membrane of Corneal Epithelium," *American Journal of Ophthalmology*, 1953, *36*, 765.

154

pure proteins from blood serum and other complex solutions. A year later the Foundation made a grant to Columbia University for aid to the research of Dr. Harold A. Abramson, an allergist and physicochemist working in the Department of Physiology of the College of Physicians and Surgeons on purification of allergens by electrophoresis.* Dr. Abramson and Dr. Moore collaborated in the University's Electrophoresis Laboratory, and Dr. Abramson spent several weeks of each summer during the next three years, with Foundation help, pursuing his studies in the laboratories of the Long Island Biological Association at Cold Spring Harbor.

Resuming his work on allergens after the war, Dr. Abramson has added other techniques, such as chemical extraction and ultraviolet spectrography, to his experiments and has kept in touch with the work of Dr. Moore. The two investigators have achieved the isolation of a colorless component from ragweed pollen that appears to be the antigen responsible for the allergic symptoms of hay fever and asthma. They have named the component trifidin. Collaborating physicians are testing the value of this and other antigens in the prevention and treatment of allergic symptoms. The purification techniques are being extended to the pollens of other plants with the hope of increasing the effectiveness of prevention and treatment of allergic distress produced by them.

The Foundation has made grants for the support of Dr. Abramson's studies from 1951 to the fall of 1955.

## Toxicology and Metabolism of Alcohol

A problem in biochemistry that has baffled investigators for many years is the process by which the body utilizes alcohol as a food stuff. Now that the tracer techniques make it possible to follow the course of ethyl alcohol in the body, new studies of the problem should be profitable.

---

* Dr. Abramson had been studying the mechanism of skin reactivity to allergens at Mt. Sinai Hospital with Foundation assistance.

Dr. Corneille Heymans, Professor of Pharmacology and Director of the J. F. Heymans Institute of the University of Ghent in Belgium, whose investigations of the nervous control of circulation and respiration were aided by the Foundation in the 1930's,* is directing research into the toxicology and metabolism of alcohol. He and a number of young scientists in his laboratory are using alcohol labelled by isotopes of carbon and hydrogen to find out how the organism is able to eliminate or to metabolize ethyl alcohol and in what tissues and organs the body stores or utilizes it. The Foundation made a two-year grant to the University of Ghent in the fall of 1953 to assist the project.

### Nuclear Physics

In 1933, the officers of the Foundation learned of a recent discovery with impressive potentialities, though at the time few could have imagined the full extent of those potentialities. A professor of physics at the University of California, Dr. Ernest O. Lawrence, had invented a machine called the cyclotron. With the enormous electrical energy it developed, Dr. Lawrence had succeeded in generating neutron radiation by a bombardment of beryllium by swiftly moving nuclei of atoms of isotopes of hydrogen. The discovery, unpublished at the time, offered possibilities of revealing previously unknown biological effects, of opening a whole new horizon for the observation of investigators of many phenomena. The Foundation made small grants directly to the University and through the Research Corporation from 1933 to 1938 to assist Dr. Lawrence's further study of the biological effects of neutron radiation, in co-operation with his physician brother, Dr. John Lawrence, as part of a general investigation in nuclear physics. Dr. John Lawrence's studies of the effects of neutron radiation upon the laboratory personnel working around the cyclotron, made with the aid of this grant, laid the groundwork for later measures that made it possible for human beings

---

* See pages 128-129.

to work in safety in the pursuit of theoretical and applied research in nuclear physics.

The development of Dr. Lawrence's research, for which he was awarded the Nobel prize in physics in 1939, and the application of techniques growing out of it to solution of biological and medical problems are far beyond the scope of this review. In a relatively short time, the cyclotron and the atomic pile had produced radioactive isotopes of virtually all the elements of the periodic table. Isotopes of more than fifty elements are now used in experimental medicine. Many questions that have long baffled biologists and clinicians have been answered and many assumptions have been revised in the light of new knowledge. Possibilities of the biological usefulness of neutron radiation that were only a hope in 1933 have become actualities, amply rewarding the faith of those who assisted Dr. Lawrence in the early stages of his research and development. The Foundation is gratified to have played even a small part in this assistance.

# RESUME OF RESOURCES AND EXPENDITURES

MRS. LADD's initial gift to the Josiah Macy, Jr. Foundation was five million dollars, of which only the income could be appropriated. Because depression conditions promptly reduced the income from the endowment, Mrs. Ladd began in 1931 to make additional gifts to supplement the Foundation's resources. During the next decade she continued to give substantial sums. They were put into a fund called "Mrs. Ladd's Special Account," now amounting to a little more than one million dollars, both income and principal of which can be used. On her death, Mrs. Ladd left the Foundation approximately thirteen million dollars, bringing her total gifts to nineteen million. The present value of the endowment is well in excess of twenty-eight million.

During the twenty-five years since 1930, the Foundation has spent the following amounts:

| | |
|---|---:|
| Grants-in-aid (842 projects) | $4,268,388.45 |
| Operational activities: | |
| Exploration, planning, and conferences, 1930-1941 | 92,328.07 |
| Exploration, planning, and conferences, 1942-1947* | 150,236.15 |
| Reprint distribution service, 1943-1945 | 201,355.13 |
| Conference program, 1948-1954 | 733,750.65 |
| Conferences, 1948-1954† | 93,646.55 |
| Exploration, planning, and other operations, 1948-1954 | 85,098.14 |

---

* The many war-time conferences and activities in co-operation with government agencies account for this great increase.

† This item includes special, or ad hoc, conferences arranged and managed by the Foundation, not meetings assisted by grants to sponsoring institutions.

The foregoing chapters contain an account of the major purposes and activities of the Josiah Macy, Jr. Foundation, not by any means a complete catalogue of the projects it has assisted, of the scientists it has considered worthy of aid, or of the operations conducted by its officers. The Directors and executives who have served the Foundation in the twenty-five years of its history have been challenged and encouraged by the wisdom of their donor, the clarity of her instructions, and her faith in the contributions that a liberally-endowed, unfettered foundation could make to human welfare.

Through years of financial depression, through a great war and the uneasy period since its end, the Foundation has used its resources for the advancement of knowledge in medical and social sciences, for the integration of the knowledge possessed by specialists in many branches of those sciences, for bringing workers in divergent areas together for co-operation and mutual understanding, for improvement of human relations. Its work has been done within the partnership between endowed foundation and university — a partnership through which the foundation, a relative newcomer to the field of learning, joins the ages-old university to add to the store of knowledge, to encourage scholarship, and to safeguard the freedom of scholars in their search for truth.

Success in such efforts is not easy to measure, or even to define. The Directors and officers of the Foundation submit this partial record with the hope that the reader may understand the purposes of their efforts in a task that will never be finished, but will constantly take on new meaning and proceed in new directions.

# ARTICLES OF INCORPORATION

WE, THE UNDERSIGNED, desiring to form a charitable corporation under and by virtue of the provisions of the Membership Corporations Law of the State of New York, do hereby make, subscribe and acknowledge this certificate as follows:

*First*: The name of the proposed Corporation is the "Josiah Macy, Jr. Foundation."

*Second*: The purposes for which it is to be formed are:

(a) The application to charitable purposes of the income of such property as the Corporation may from time to time possess, including the giving of the same to any other charitable corporation or corporations;

(b) The application to charitable purposes of the income of such property as the Corporation may from time to time possess to initiate, stimulate, develop and support scientific investigations of the fundamental aspects of health, of sickness, and of methods for the relief of suffering. As means to these ends the Corporation may aid and cooperate with and receive the aid and cooperation of other existing or future similar agencies and undertakings which to it may seem necessary, advisable or convenient in the accomplishment of any of its purposes; and

(c) In case of property acquired by gift, devise, or bequest, the application of the income and the principal thereof to such charitable purposes as the Donor or Testator shall have prescribed in the instrument of gift or in his will,

(d) The Corporation will not engage in any of the activities mentioned in subdivision 1, of section 11 of the Membership Corporations Law, without first extending the purposes pursuant to section 30 of the Membership Corporations Law and procuring the approval of the Department of Social Welfare.

*Third*: The territory in which these operations are principally to be conducted is the United States of America, but it shall not be restricted thereto.

*Fourth*: The City and County in which its office is to be located are the City and County of New York.

161

*Fifth*: The number of its Directors shall be fifteen.

*Sixth*: The names and places of residence of the Directors of the Corporation until the first annual meeting are:

      \*      \*      \*      \*      \*      \*      \*      \*

*Seventh*: All of the subscribers to this certificate are of full age; at least two-thirds of them are citizens of the United States; at least one of them is a resident of the State of New York, and of the persons named as Directors, at least one is a citizen of the United States and a resident of the State of New York.

*Eighth*: No Director or other officer of this Corporation shall receive directly or indirectly any salary, compensation or emolument from such Corporation except reasonable compensation for services in effecting one or more of its corporate purposes, all as provided for in the said Membership Corporations Law.

*Ninth*: The Directors may provide for the appointment of individual or corporate trustees of any or all of its property and confer on such trustees such of the powers, duties or obligations of the Directors of such corporation in relation to the care, custody or management of such property as may be deemed advisable, and also for the manner of appointment of their successors.

IN WITNESS WHEREOF we have hereunto set our hands and seals in duplicate the 19th day of April, Nineteen Hundred and Thirty.

| | |
|---|---|
| VALENTINE E. MACY, JR. | LUDWIG KAST |
| DAVE H. MORRIS | FREDERICK J. FAULKS |
| | LAWRENCE MORRIS | |

# INDEX

Cohn, Alfred E , 66
Cold injury
  conference group on, 24, 146-147, 148
  studies of, 147-148
Cold stress, relation of adrenal cortex to, 123
Columbia-Presbyterian Medical Center
  exchange program, 48-49
  Neurological Institute, 71-72, 145
  Normal Child Development Clinic, 71-72
  School of Public Health and Administrative Medicine, 61
  Department of Tropical Medicine, 47
Columbia University
  College of Physicians and Surgeons, 28, 30-31, 32, 33, 36, 38, 46-47, 52, 65, 68, 69, 80, 81, 82-83, 118, 119, 120, 125, 135, 145, 154-155
  Research Division at Goldwater Memorial Hospital, 52, 84
  Department of Sociology, 56
  Department of Zoology, 73
  Teachers College, 65
Commission on Graduate Medical Education, 46
Commission on Medical Education; see Association of American Medical Colleges
Committee on Costs of Medical Care, 55
Committee on Medical Research of the Office of Research and Development; see United States government
Communication, Foundation interest in, 17, 21, 22, 24, 40-41, 95-96, 98-99, 99-100, 110-111, 160; see also Conference technique
Community Service Society, 56, 68
Conference groups, list of, 24-25
Conference of Consultants on Services to Children in Germany, 105
Conference program, 13-25, 52, 100, 159
Conference technique, 14, 16, 17, 18, 19, 20, 24, 109, 110-111, 113-114, 115, 144, 146

*Conferences on Drug Addiction Among Adolescents*, 116
Conferences, transactions of, 21-24, 146
Connective tissues, diseases of
  conference group on, 24, 84, 86, 149
Convalescence; see Bone and wound healing; Metabolic aspects of convalescence
*Convalescence and Rehabilitation, Proceedings of the Conference . . . 1944*, 56
*Convalescent Care, Proceedings of the Conference . . . 1939*, 56
Cope, Oliver, 39
Copenhagen, University of
  Biochemistry Institute, 140
Corneal basement membrane, 154
Cornell University, 93
  Behavior Farm, 67, 93-95
  Medical College, 29, 35, 36, 56, 66, 67, 68, 118, 119, 120, 121, 130-132, 140, 148, 152-153
Cortisone, see Adrenal cortex; Adrenocorticotropic hormone
Council of Teaching Hospitals, 51-52
Cowdry, Edmund V., 14, 25, 80, 82
Cushing, Harvey, 118
Cybernetics
  conference group on, 20-21, 24, 99
*Cybernetics*, 21
Cyclotron, invention of, 156

### D

Dam, Henrik, 140
Davies, J. N. P., 141
Davis, Hallowell, 66
Delinquency, 68-69
Deutsch, Felix, 67
Dewey, Evelyn (Mrs. Granville M. Smith), 72
Dewey, John, ix
Dougherty, Thomas F., 122
Dragstedt, Lester R., 118-119
Drug addiction in adolescents
  conferences on, 115-116
Dunbar, H. Flanders, 65
Dunn, Leslie C., 73

Gutman, Alexander B., 31
Guy's Hospital, London, 48-49
Gyorgy, Paul, 24, 28, 29, 79, 130, 137, 142-144

**H**

Hadley, Hamilton, ix
Hahn, Paul F., 136-137
Hall, G. E., 127
Hanover Bank, The, vii
Harrison, Tinsley R., 129-130
Harrower, Molly R., 36, 86
Harvard University, 27, 36
  Biological Laboratories, 73, 139
  Graduate School of Business Administration, Department of Industrial Research, 38
  Medical School, 30, 34, 38, 39, 47, 53, 66, 67, 75, 76, 93, 127, 129, 140
Haus Schwalbach, conference at, 110
Hayes, Mark A, 85
Health and human relations in Germany, conferences on
  Princeton, N. J., 104-107, 108, 109, 111, 113
  Williamsburg, Va., 107, 108, 109, 111
  Hiddesen, Western Germany, 107-110, 111
*Health and Human Relations in Germany*
  Princeton conference report, 106-107
  Williamsburg conference report, 108
  Hiddesen conference report, 109, 111
Health Insurance Plan of Greater New York, 56
Health services, administration of, *see* Administrative medicine
Health team, the, 57-58, 60, 103
*Healthy Personality Development in Children*, 114
Heart and circulation, studies of, 124-128, *see also* Arteriosclerosis; Hypertension; Problems of aging
  capillary circulation, 28, 29, 130, 131
Heat, human acclimatization to, 38
Herrick, C. Judson, 91n

Heymans, Corneille, 52, 128-129, 156
Hiddesen, conference at; *see* Health and human relations in Germany, conferences on
High Commissioner for Western Germany; *see* United States government, Department of State
Hill, Kenneth R., 142
Hoagland, Hudson, 25, 121
Hoet, Joseph-Pierre, 76
Hoffman, Ruth S, 35
Holbrook, William Paul, 24, 30, 86
Hoppin, William W., ix
Horvath, Steven M., 147-148
Hoskins, Roy G., 25
Hospital, functions of, 58-60
Hospital survey for New York, 55
Human relations, 89-116; *see also* Health and human relations in Germany
  conference on clinical approaches to, 13-14
  conference on human relations in the family, 14
Hypertension, studies of, 119, 128-134
Hypnosis, 68
*Hypnotherapy, A Survey of the Literature*, 68

**I**

Illinois, University of
  College of Medicine, 140
  Illinois Neuropsychiatric Institute, 98
Institut de Biologie Physico-Chimique, Paris, 152-153
Institute of Administrative Medicine; *see* Columbia-Presbyterian Medical Center, School of Public Health and Administrative Medicine
Insurance, medical and health; *see* Prepayment for medical and hospital care
Integration of knowledge, Foundation interest in, 5, 6, 9, 11, 43-44, 55, 71, 77, 99, 117, 132, 160
Interagency Conference on Children, 113-114

U

Union of American Biological Societies, 14, 82
United Hospital Fund of New York, 55
United Nations, 101-102, 103
Economic and Social Council, 102
Food and Agriculture Organization, 143-144
United Nations Children's Fund, 102
United Nations Educational, Scientific, and Cultural Organization, 102, 104
World Health Organization, 96, 97, 102, 104, 143-144
Study Group on the Psychobiological Development of the Child, 91
United States government
support of medical research, 7-8
Army, 38, 39, 40
Chemical Warfare Service, Technical Division, 32, 33
Signal Corps, 38
Surgeon General's Office, 38-39, 40
Army Air Force, 30-31, 100
Air Surgeon, 30-31, 32, 37, 40
Department of Health, Education, and Welfare
Children's Bureau, 105, 113, 114-115
Office of Education, 108
Department of State, 41, 105, 107, 111
Educational Exchanges Service, 110
Foreign Service conferences, 100
Office of German Public Affairs, 111
Office of the High Commissioner for Western Germany, 105-106, 108
Interdepartmental Committee on Children and Youth, 113-114
Navy, 31, 39
Surgeon General, 40
Office of Civil Defense, 116
Office of Research and Development
Committee on Medical Research, 7, 39
Office of War Information, 41
Public Health Service, 37, 68, 104
Hygienic Laboratory, 7

United States government—*Cont'd*
National Heart Institute, 149
Section on Gerontology, 87
National Institute of Mental Health, 95, 105
National Institutes of Health, 7-8
Unit on Gerontology, 85, 87
Selective Service System, 35, 36, 38
Veterans Administration, 37, 38, 86, 99
War Department, 32, 33
War Shipping Administration, 37
United States Sanitary Commission, 40
University, the, in relation to the endowed foundation, 7, 8-9, 160
University College of the West Indies, 142-144
Urey, Harold C., 81
Urist, Marshall R., 149-150

V

Valk, Margaret A. (Thomas), 59n
Vanderbilt University
School of Medicine, 30, 129, 136-137
Vassar College, 77
Veterans Administration, see United States government
Villinger, Werner, 108
Virchow, Rudolf, 63
Vision, chemistry and mechanism of, 139-140
Vitamins; see also Nutrition
A, 139-140
B, 122-124, 139, 140
C, 139-140
E, 140
K, 140
P, 138-139

W

Wake Forest College
Bowman Gray School of Medicine, 30, 83-84
Wald, George, 139-140
War, medical research in relation to; see National defense, medical problems of
*War Neuroses in North Africa*, 37

JOSIAH MACY JR. FOUNDATION

Washington University
   School of Medicine, 67
Waterlow, J. C., 144n
Watson, Cecil J., 25
Weiskotten, H G, 47, 59n
Weiss, Soma, 129
Welfare Council of New York City
   (now Welfare and Health
   Council of New York City),
   55
   Committee on the Use of Narcotics
      Among Teen-Age Youth, 115
Western Germany; see Health and
   human relations in Germany,
   conferences on
Western Reserve University
   School of Medicine, 28, 38, 125-
   126, 129
White, Abraham, 122, 124
White House Conference on Chil-
   dren, see Midcentury White
   House Conference on Children
   and Youth
Whitehorn, John C., 78-79
Wiener, Norbert, 20n, 21
Wilkins, Lawson, 78
Willets, J. Macy, ix, xi
Wisconsin, University of, 36
Wislocki, George, 24

Wistar Institute of Anatomy and
   Biology, 72
Wolf, Stewart, 67
Wolff, Harold G., 36, 66, 67
Woodruff, I. Ogden, v
Worcester Foundation for Experi-
   mental Biology, 74, 121
World Federation for Mental Health,
   101-104, 105, 108, 110
World Health Organization; see
   United Nations
*World Mental Health* (formerly,
   *Bulletin of the World Federa-
   tion for Mental Health*) 103,
   104
Wright, David G., 25
Wright, Irving S., 24, 125

Y

Yale University
   Institute of Human Relations, 14,
   66, 77
   School of Medicine, 30, 52-53, 75,
   76, 85, 118, 120, 121, 122

Z

Zweifach, Benjamin W., 28, 29, 130,
   131, 134

Printed in the USA
CPSIA information can be obtained
at www.ICGtesting.com
LVHW020801120424
777131LV00003B/524